The Hundred Dresses

ALSO BY ERIN MCKEAN

The Hundred Dresses

The Most Iconic Styles of Our Time

ERIN MCKEAN

ILLUSTRATED BY **DONNA MEHALKO**

B L O O M S B U R Y

NEW YORK · LONDON · NEW DELHI · SYDNEY

Text © 2013 by Erin McKean
Illustrations © 2013 by Donna Mehalko

The excerpt on page 81 is from Marcel Proust's
Remembrance of Things Past (trans. Charles
Kenneth Scott-Moncrieff).

Published by Bloomsbury Publishing, London, New Delhi,
New York, Sydney
Bloomsbury USA, 175 Fifth Avenue, New York, NY 10010
Bloomsbury Publishing Plc, 50 Bedford Square, London
WC1B 3DP

All papers used by Bloomsbury Publishing are natural,
recyclable products made from wood grown in well-managed
forests. The manufacturing processes conform to the environmental
regulations of the country of origin.

Library of Congress Cataloging-in-Publication Data
McKean, Erin.
  The hundred dresses : the most iconic styles of our time / Erin McKean ;
illustrated by Donna Mehalko.
     p. cm.
ISBN: 978-1-60819-976-1 (hardback US)
  1. Dresses. 2. Women's clothing. 3. Fashion design. I. Title.
  GT2060.M35 2013
  391.4'72—dc23
                      2012043594

A CIP catalogue record for this book is available from the British Library
ISBN: 978-1-4081-9050-0 (hardback UK)

First edition published in Great Britain and the United States in 2013

1 3 5 7 9 10 8 6 4 2

Book design by Kimberly Glyder
Printed in China by South China Printing Company, Dongguan, Guangdong

For all the readers of www.dressaday.com all over the world, who have left insightful comments, sent intriguing links, enabled my fabric-buying habit to a shameful degree, and shared my passion for Airship Hostess dresses— this book is especially for you.

Contents

Introduction

In the classic children's book *The Hundred Dresses*, by Eleanor Estes, Wanda Petronski is bullied for saying she has "a hundred dresses—all lined up in my closet." The book is supposed to be about bullying (published in 1944, the book makes Wanda's poverty and Polish last name an issue as well), but when I first read it, all I could think of was—what did the dresses look like? There's mention of "a pale blue one with cerise-colored trimmings" and "a brilliant jungle green with a red sash," but the other ninety-eight are left to the reader's imagination.

Wanda is persecuted by the other girls for saying she has a hundred dresses—no one could ever have a hundred dresses, they think—until they realize that Wanda's imagination (bigger than any closet) could hold a hundred dresses and more.

All of our imaginations can hold a hundred dresses or more—not just variations of color and fabric and trimmings, shape and line, but distinct species of dresses that we recognize and distinguish as easily as we differentiate between daisies and daffodils. We can say "That's a June Cleaver dress" or "She was wearing a kind of Flamenco-y thing" and feel confident we'll be understood.

And it's not just when we're talking about these dresses—we know (or think we know) what we're saying with them when we wear them. We are different women, almost, in a Garden Party dress than we are in the Siren (even if we're wearing them with all the same people who have known us forever). We know what's being communicated by a Marilyn halter versus a Mary Quant mini, what people read into a Bandage dress or a Dirndl.

I'm sure other garments have their semiotics as well (there must be at least a dissertation, if not a book, on the subtle distinctions between plus-fours, knickers, and pantaloons), but dresses, being inherently feminine, are somehow more expressive. Dresses, perhaps because they are the only outer garment exclusively identified with women, are somehow more emphatic in their communication. Dresses seem to have a wider vocabulary in which to express all the things that women can be, and they are exuberant in that expressiveness. Dresses roll their sartorial *r*'s when speaking the language of clothes.

These dresses also have stories—all good archetypes do, even if the details of those stories have been blurred by time. By wearing these dresses you insert yourself into the narratives they inhabit. The story of someone wearing the Siren dress is a different story altogether from that of the wearer of the Japanese Fashion, but both wearers are hoping for some kind of happy ending.

The hundred dresses here aren't all the dress archetypes in the world, by a long shot, but they're ones that are referenced frequently and worn consistently. Some are seen more frequently and consistently than others—on days when I see one of the rarer examples (it's not every day you see someone togged out in a Fortuny or a J. Lo) I feel like a bird-watcher who's just added an entry to her life list—but all of them have significance, the kind that T-shirts and jeans just can't match.

In addition to calling out these dresses as archetypes, I've tried to include where applicable the appropriate accessories and notable wearers, as well as the (ir)responsible designers. The lists of wearers and designers are meant to be suggestive rather than exhaustive—a list of everyone semifamous who's ever worn a Cheongsam or a Slip dress would run the length of the phone book, if people had phone books anymore.

You can use this book as a field guide, to help you spot dress tropes; you can use it as an instruction manual, to help you decide what stories you want to embody; or you can use it (as the labels on everything fun say) "for entertainment purposes only."

Whether you save dresses for special occasions or wear them every day, I hope this field guide to frocks helps you become even more fluent in the language of clothes.

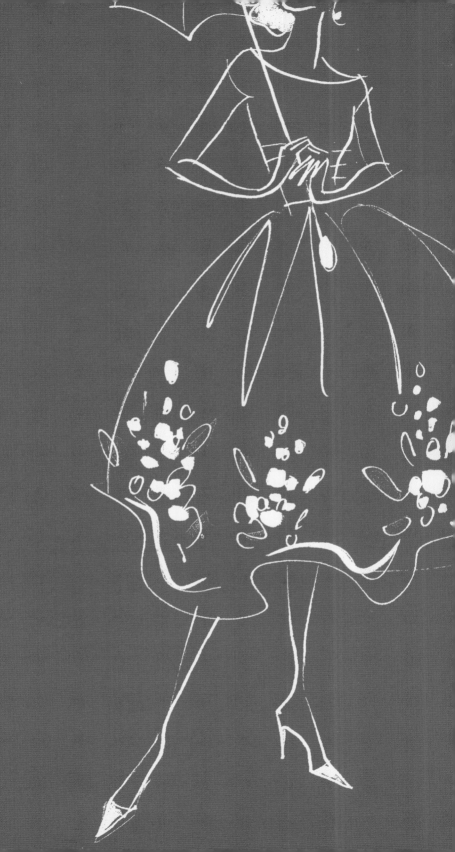

THE ADDICTED TO LOVE

WE'VE ALL SEEN THE 1986 video: Robert Palmer, in a simple white shirt and black tie, clutches a microphone for dear life while five terrifying women in high-necked, long-sleeved (and slightly sheer, much to the delight of MTV-watching teenage boys everywhere) black minidresses surround him and dance robotically while pretending to play instruments.

The Addicted to Love dress is any dress that essentially sets out to turn you into a prop, a backdrop, stage dressing, or scenery, especially if it does so in a hyper-sexualized way. Modern rap videos employ the same methods (only with much less fabric), and it can be argued that the bridesmaid's dress is a tamer version of this phenomenon.

The Addicted to Love differs from a uniform—a uniform is intended to encourage team spirit and fellow feeling in addition to providing a consistent appearance to outsiders. The Addicted to Love, in all its variants, is concerned with the audience only. No one seems to be worried about a unit cohesion problem among backup dancers.

When you're wearing the Addicted to Love, either by choice or by coercion, it's best to give yourself fully over to it. Wear it like a costume (which, of course, it is) and throw yourself into the role, whether it's fembot, handmaiden, conference-booth staffer, or video vixen. If you can cultivate a fine appreciation of absurdity, that will help tremendously.

ACCESSORIES: Sheer black stockings and stiletto heels, slicked-back hair, dramatic smoky-eye makeup, and shiny red lipstick on a mouth that never smiles.

RELATED: The Bandage dress.

WORN BY: The models in the original video were Julia Bolino, Kathy Davies, Mak Gilchrist, Patty Kelly, and Julie Pankhurst. (Also referenced by Beyoncé and her Single Ladies, although they were much more foreground than background.)

THE AIRSHIP HOSTESS

2

THE AIRSHIP HOSTESS DRESS is not for present-day flight attendants or even stewardesses; it is a purely notional dress for an alternative history where giant cruise-ship-like dirigibles float through the skies, doing the still-exotic New York–San Francisco run at a leisurely 135 mph.

The Airship Hostess dress is vaguely 1930s, vaguely 1940s, but with a distinctly official air. There are useful pockets (usually asymmetrical); there are buttons (usually asymmetrical); there's a long, narrow skirt and a little collar and definitely something pointy and art-deco-y going on. It's worn bareheaded or with a jaunty little hat, and purses or bags are not carried while on duty (that's what the pockets are for). Dickies and gloves? Optional.

The women in the Airship Hostess dresses are the heroines of screwball comedies: they're heiresses running away from their inheritances, grifters on the make (with hearts of gold), dames both dizzy and hard-bitten. They have secrets; they have repartee; they do their before-takeoff safety briefing as a patter song. They always fall in love on their voyages, either with the poor boy in steerage (who is often a prince in disguise) or with the older, world-weary war correspondent, or occasionally with the semisloshed and semilouche lounge piano player.

Even though modern airships are limited to thrill rides and hovering over major sporting events (yawn), the Airship Hostess dress is not. It's amazing how competent a trim, tailored, functional dress—one that isn't trying to be a man's suit—can make you feel. The Airship Hostess is prepared for any disaster on the ground or in the skies (short of a full-on *Hindenburg*), and you can be, too.

ACCESSORIES: A swagger stick (for captains and above).

WORN BY: The Airship Hostess dress seems to be worn mostly by the women illustrated on home sewing patterns.

3

THE AMISH DRESS is part of a tradition of plain-dress clothing primarily followed by Anabaptists and other religious groups. The stereotypical version of this dress is long-sleeved and dark in color, with a defined waist and long fullish skirt, but the adjective *Amish* is often used for any long unadorned dress. A plain dress is a simple one without too much decoration; "plain dress" (often capitalized by adherents) is any clothing selected to prioritize utility, modesty, long wear, and inconspicuousness.

Plain dress spans a continuum, ranging from more or less conventionally dressed people who refuse to wear anything with a logo to people who regularly dress in a personal "uniform" (think Diana Vreeland, who was anything but plain, but who wore the same dress over and over, just made in different fabrics) and those who disdain corporate-made, disposable, fast-fashion clothing, as well as those who follow a divinely appointed dress code.

One of the main reasons to wear plain clothing is that it removes the obligation many women feel to be alluring. Replacing perceived social pressure with a religious or philosophical one (not all wearers of simple dress are religious) means never having to be buffeted by the capricious whims of fashion. (Compare the consistent and unchanging customs of the various plain-dress sects with the rapid-fire style changes of the design-conscious.) A woman in a plain dress is never inappropriately dressed for any event; the notion is nonsensical. She is a conscientious objector in the modern war over how women's bodies are perceived. (Of course, this assumes that the wearing of plain dress is a free choice and not compelled by the threat of violence, ostracism, or shunning.)

ACCESSORIES: A shawl or apron, a bonnet or cap, and the courage of one's convictions.

WORN BY: Women of various religious groups, including the Amish, Brethren, Hutterites, some Quakers and Mennonites, and Hasidic and Haredi Jews; also women involved in anticonsumerist and other simplicity movements.

THE ANNE SHIRLEY

THE ANNE SHIRLEY (also known as the Anne of Green Gables) is, strictly speaking, any dress with huge, puffed, leg-o'-mutton sleeves.

In the classic children's book *Anne of Green Gables*, Anne, an orphan, comes to live with Matthew and Marilla Cuthbert, a brother and sister who run a small farm on Prince Edward Island. They had sent for a boy to help with the farm work but got Anne by mistake and (against their better judgment) decide to keep her. Anne, sensitive, romantic, and imaginative, is disappointed with the serviceable and plain dresses Marilla makes for her to replace the skimpy orphanage issue; she has her heart set on fashionable puffed sleeves so wide you have to "go through a door sideways." She feels the lack of puffed sleeves sorely but makes up her mind to let her imagination do the work . . . until her first Christmas at Green Gables, when quiet Matthew surprises her with the dress of her dreams.

> Oh, how pretty it was—a lovely soft brown gloria with all the gloss of silk; a skirt with dainty frills and shirrings; a waist elaborately pintucked in the most fashionable way, with a little ruffle of filmy lace at the neck. But the sleeves—they were the crowning glory! Long elbow cuffs, and above them two beautiful puffs divided by rows of shirring and bows of brown silk ribbon.

The Anne Shirley is any dress you want with all your heart and soul, any dress you wish for without hope of fulfillment, and especially any dress that, against all odds, becomes yours. Puffed sleeves optional.

ACCESSORIES: A full heart, gratitude.

WORN BY: Everyone, someday.

THE ARTIST'S SMOCK

5

AS EVERYONE KNOWS, the actual production—the "doing"—of art is a messy, painful, tedious, and difficult business; it can be emotionally and intellectually rewarding, but not nearly as instantly rewarding as the "being" of art, as being seen as an artist. And since many of the other visible, stereotypical markers of artist status (standing awkwardly holding a glass of wine while appearing not to be eavesdropping on gallery-goers, staring abstractedly into space during conversations, writing completely opaque "statements") are more difficult to comprehend in a single glance, artists have the smock, much in the same way that architects—who suffer from similar problems—wear unusual eyeglasses.

So it's not surprising that the Artist's Smock, the universal shorthand signifier of "pretty female artist," is often worn as a dress, by artists and nonartists alike. In fact, it is probably more often worn as a dress than as an artist's cover-up—modern-day artists don't normally wear the classic round-collared smock, tending instead to favor boiler suits and other overallsy garments, or jeans that can become suitably paint-splattered and cool.

ACCESSORIES: A perfectly placed smudge of paint on one cheekbone, an intent expression, a classic wooden palette, a garret room (with north light if possible). Beret optional. For wearers under ten years old, the artist's smock is appliquéd with paintbrushes.

RELATED: The Baby Doll.

THE AUSTEN

6

THE AUSTEN DRESS—more properly known as the Empire, Directoire, or Regency dress—is high-waisted, with a soft, fairly unstructured skirt (especially when compared with the panniers of the preceding eras). The neck and décolletage are left bare, and the sleeves are short. The classic Austen dress is made of soft, sheer muslin in white or another light color.

The purpose of the Austen dress is to imagine oneself as a Jane Austen heroine, preferably Elizabeth from *Pride and Prejudice*: witty, intelligent, of a "lively, playful disposition," and, of course, the eventual partner of Mr. Darcy. The Austen dress is probably one of the most wearable of period costumes, in that it requires comparatively little fabric and few special undergarments.

But the compelling romance of the Austen dress sometimes overshadows what is truly remarkable in the character of Elizabeth, the heroine inside it: her "liveliness of mind" does not make her dissatisfied. In fact, Austen writes, "It was her business to be satisfied—and certainly her temper to be happy." She does not let herself be cast too far down by the slights she receives, but focuses on others (including her sister Jane and her father) and on the inherent absurdity of the situations she finds herself in. Being able to laugh at one's circumstances and enjoy life as it comes promises a better life, in the end, than even the most advantageous marriage.

ACCESSORIES: Various capes, shawls, coats, and jackets (including mantelets, spencers, redingotes, and pelisses), spirit, soft low shoes, a reticule, and Mr. Darcy (or equivalent).

WORN BY: Just about every British actress, at one time or another.

THE BABY DOLL

7

THE BABY DOLL DRESS has a high waist and full short skirt, and is often embellished with bows or lace trim, especially at the waist. It is sleeveless or has short sleeves (in extreme examples, it has short puffed sleeves), a deep scooped neck, and occasionally a Peter Pan collar. The Baby Doll dress appears to best advantage in white or light colors, especially pink, blue, lavender, and yellow, although it may be color-blocked with a black bodice.

The purpose of the Baby Doll dress is to look infantilized and sexualized at the same time: the focus on the breasts and legs, while obscuring the waist, makes the wearer look younger, the size of the breasts notwithstanding. The technical term for this is *pedomorphism* (yep, that sounds terrible, doesn't it?), "the retention by the adult organism of infantile or juvenile characteristics." One of the "juvenile characteristics" that the Baby Doll dress emphasizes is having legs longer than your arms; by hiding the waist, the Baby Doll exaggerates the length of the legs.

ACCESSORIES: Mary Janes, a small top-handled handbag or a clutch, shiny lip gloss, copious false eyelashes, the propensity to call unrelated grown men "Daddy."

RELATED: The Classic Party Dress, the Artist's Smock.

WORN BY: Twiggy, Zooey Deschanel, Kate Middleton.

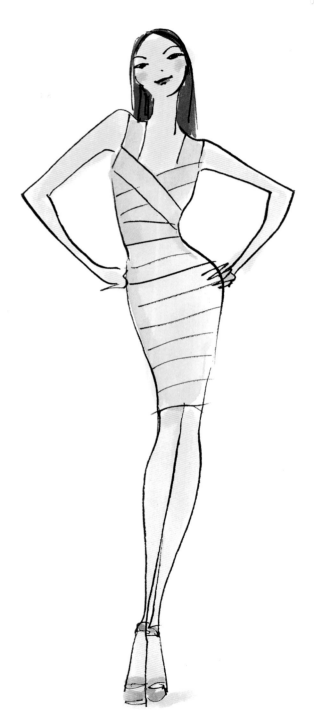

THE BANDAGE DRESS

8

THE CLASSIC BANDAGE DRESS, made famous by Hervé Léger (and, to a lesser extent, by Azzedine Alaïa), is a short, tight, formfitting dress that is usually constructed of wide bands of elastic. In black, white, metallic, or bright colors, often with asymmetrical detailing or cutouts, the Bandage dress was a staple of 1980s supermodel chic—and usually requires a supermodel figure to pull off.

The message of the Bandage dress is simple: "Look on my bod, ye mighty, and despair." The Bandage dress is designed primarily to communicate sex appeal and the power that comes from sex appeal. The secondary message is that of candor: the wearer of the Bandage dress has nothing to hide—in fact, cannot hide. The Bandage dress has no pockets and usually allows for few, if any, undergarments. What you see is what you get.

When wearing a Bandage dress, you must not let the slightest flicker of doubt cross your mind. You are confident, you are strong, and you are willing to throw your cell phone, as hard as you can, at the head of anyone who even thinks about crossing you. Wearing a Bandage dress is not for the faint of heart or for second-guessers.

The natural habitat of the Bandage dress is late nights at the A-list party, especially the A-list fashion party, but it is rarely seen on the awards-show red carpet, being too much like braggadocio for events where likability is more important than displays of power.

ACCESSORIES: Skyscraper-high heels, a clutch (especially a bejeweled minaudière), a limo, and, if possible, a very, very rich man.

RELATED: The Addicted to Love.

WORN BY: Naomi Campbell (classic), Blake Lively (modern).

THE BEAUXHEMIAN

9

THE BEAUXHEMIAN DRESS—sometimes called fauxhemian—is usually long, flowing, in an "ethnic" print, and very, very expensive. It can be cotton but is more usually silk.

The point of wearing a Beauxhemian dress is to look as if you do not care about money and status at all while projecting that you are, in truth, wealthy and elite. It is extremely difficult to pull off the Beauxhemian look if you work a nine-to-five job (and want to look as if you care about it). It is possible to be a weekend Beauxhemian (easier if you live in a warm climate), but the full Beauxhemian is better suited to artistic or semiartistic pursuits, especially modeling, which gives you access both to expensive Beauxhemian gowns and to the slim figure that makes them look even more expensive than they are.

ACCESSORIES: Long hair (preferably wavy), dangly earrings, a leather saddlebag, flat jeweled sandals, something Cartier, a private jet, a tan from Tulum or Ibiza (or better yet, someone's private island).

RELATED: The Flower Child Bride.

WORN BY: Nicole Richie, Kate Moss, Sienna Miller, trustifarians everywhere.

DESIGNERS: Roberto Cavalli, Max Azria, Philip Lim, Erin Fetherston, Temperley.

THE BIOHAZARD

THE BIOHAZARD DRESS has many different shapes and forms: an effective Biohazard dress could be made of garbage (sometimes called "trashion"), raw meat, five-inch razor-sharp spikes, even (once the technology allows) harnessed swarms of live bees. The connecting thread is the threat of more or less imminent peril to the wearer and bystanders.

Wearers of Biohazard dresses are usually performance artists of one kind or another. The idea is to take the dress, something that is pretty and feminine, and turn it into a disturbing death trap.

The Biohazard has much in common with the Stunt dress and with dresses worn by Lady Gaga (Lady Gaga being one of the main wearers of the Biohazard dress). But where the Stunt dress is focused on the event being attended and Lady Gaga's dresses focus on, well, being Lady Gaga, the Biohazard is really all about evoking feelings of disgust and fear, if not causing actual injury.

The ideal outcome for a Biohazard dress wearer is to send bystanders to the local hospital to be treated for shock and possibly dehydration, or, at the very least, to be ejected from the venue by the local health department.

ACCESSORIES: A lack of concern for human life, a Tesla-coil headdress, latex gloves (for your stylist).

RELATED: The Swan.

WORN BY: Czech Canadian artist Jana Sterbak (who wore the original meat dress in 1987).

DESIGNERS: Alexander McQueen, Hussein Chalayan.

THE BOND GIRL **11**

ALTHOUGH MANY OF THE ICONIC images of the women known as "Bond girls" involve the skimpiest of bikinis, the women in 007's cinematic life are also no slouches in the evening-gown competition.

They had to be, because Bond, in addition to being a connoisseur of what's inside the dresses, has a surprisingly knowing eye for fashion. Here's how Ian Fleming describes Vesper Lynd's dress from *Casino Royale*:

> Her medium-length dress was of gray *soie sauvage* with a square-cut bodice, lasciviously tight across her fine breasts.

Later, she wears . . .

> a dress of black velvet, simple and yet with the touch of splendor that only half a dozen *couturiers* in the world can achieve. There was a thin necklace of diamonds at her throat and a diamond clip in the low vee which just exposed the jutting swell of her breasts.

You may have noticed that the operative word in both descriptions is *breasts*: despite being called "girls," the female foils that Bond battles and beds are full-grown women, and usually more than averagely endowed. The Bond Girl is a dress that makes the most of those particular projectile weapons, which, although they will set off no metal detectors and hardly ever explode, tend to disable Bond (however temporarily) more efficiently than antiaircraft missiles, lasers, or grenades.

The Bond Girl dress is all about weaponizing the cleavage. Ideally, it reduces men—or at least men of lesser mettle than Bond—to gaping stupefaction, rendering them helpless while you achieve your objective, whatever it is. The Bond Girl dress takes no prisoners. (Well, actually, it may take prisoners.)

ACCESSORIES: A name that gives twelve-year-old boys the giggles, thigh holster (gun, knife, or both—that's why you have two legs), no hesitation about jumping into bed with dangerous, enigmatic men whom you may or may not try to kill later.

WORN BY: (In the films) Honor Blackman, Diana Rigg, Barbara Bach, Talisa Soto, Halle Berry, Eva Green, and others.

DESIGNERS: The early films expended most of their energy on dressing Bond—the famous white bikini worn by Ursula Andress was put together from one of her own bras and a pair of underwear bought to match. Later movies used better-known designers, such as Roberto Cavalli (*Casino Royale*), Azzedine Alaïa (for Grace Jones in *A View to a Kill*), Donatella Versace (*Die Another Day*), and Prada (*Quantum of Solace*).

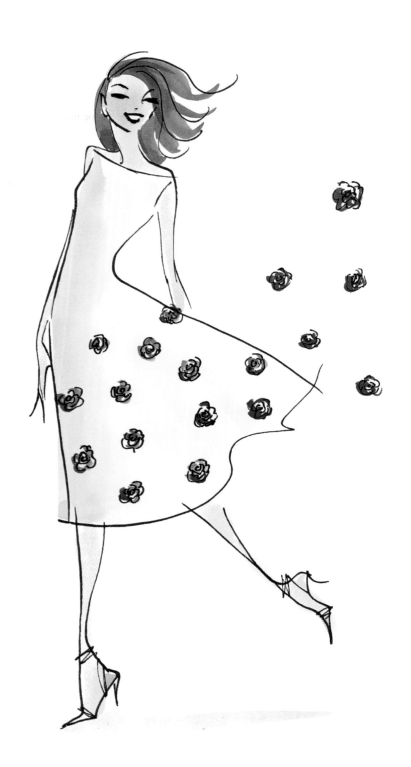

THE BOUQUET

12

THE BOUQUET DRESS may be short or long, tight or full, bare or modest, but in all its incarnations it is covered with embroidered, appliquéd, or printed flowers. Usually the flowers are more or less realistic depictions, but there are variations of the Bouquet where the flowers are abstract, deconstructed, or mere nods to the idea of blooms. It's the expanse of surface area given over to flowers that defines a Bouquet dress—one or two blossoms do not a Bouquet dress make. (Perhaps that would be called a bud vase dress?)

The Bouquet dress is meant to call to mind the traditional association of women with flowers: whether you are a shrinking violet, an exotic orchid, a full-blown rose, or as fresh as a daisy, the Bouquet dress conveys that you, too, are a beautiful miracle of nature and deserve appreciation as such.

Bouquet dresses are versatile, showing up in every possible dress class. They are fairly common as cotton summer dresses (especially sundresses), evening gowns (where tone-on-tone flowers are common), and even wedding dresses (with appliquéd daisies being a popular choice).

ACCESSORIES: Just about anything, although the wearer should be wary of overbedecking herself: flowers on the dress do not also obligate the wearer to add flowers in the hair, flowers on the shoes, or floral jewelry, to carry an actual bouquet, or to wear heavy floral perfume. (The goal is to create an association between the wearer and the beauty and freshness of flowers, not to remind onlookers forcibly of the last time they were in a florist's shop.)

WORN BY: Audrey Hepburn in *Sabrina*; Halle Berry in her Elie Saab at the Oscars.

DESIGNERS: Oscar de la Renta, Edith Head, Elie Saab, Giambattista Valli, Valentino.

THE BREAKFAST AT TIFFANY'S 13

WHEN WE FIRST SEE HOLLY GOLIGHTLY in Truman Capote's 1958 novella, "it was a warm evening, nearly summer, and she wore a slim cool black dress, black sandals, and a pearl choker."

Three dresses were made by Hubert de Givenchy for the 1961 film: one is in the Givenchy Paris archives, one is in Madrid at the Museum of Costume, and the third was sold by Christie's in December 2006 to an anonymous bidder for £410,000. Givenchy originally donated the third dress to French author Dominique Lapierre, to benefit his City of Joy Aid charity, inspired by his 1985 novel of the same name.

The Breakfast at Tiffany's dress is the eight-hundred-pound gorilla of little black dresses. It does whatever it wants, whenever it wants; it parties all night with disreputable characters (and visits them in prison) without a stain on its own, then heads downtown for breakfast. Wearing the Breakfast at Tiffany's dress telegraphs high spirits and elegance simultaneously; you are game for almost anything but somehow distanced from any hint of sordidness.

An exact replica of any of the dresses made for the film veers too close to an Audrey Hepburn Halloween costume. A Breakfast at Tiffany's dress is one that makes just a nod to the movie versions: a long narrow silhouette and a highish neckline should be enough to evoke the dress without slavishly imitating it.

ACCESSORIES: A big fake-pearl choker, a long ebony cigarette holder, a jeweled updo (with tiara), sunglasses, and a little something for the powder room. Cat optional.

RELATED: The Chanel Jersey dress.

WORN BY: Audrey Hepburn (of course), Natalie Portman (who wore the dress for the November 2006 cover of *Harper's Bazaar*).

THE BUBBLE DRESS 14

THE BUBBLE DRESS was the brainchild of designer Christian Lacroix, who show-ed the first incarnation in 1986. The Bubble was part of his last collection for the House of Patou, for which he was awarded the Dé d'Or (the Golden Thimble) by the international fashion press.

The point of the Bubble dress is to be wildly impractical in a sexy way. With its close-fitting bodice and huge colorful short skirt, the Bubble (also called the Pouf or the Bouffant) emphasizes the legs, cleavage, and bank balance of the wearer.

The Bubble dress was—like all bubbles, sadly—destined to pop after just a short time. But while it lasted, it was not only what *InStyle* editor Hal Rubenstein called "a ball gown stuffed into a minidress" but also as fun and as effervescent as the champagne its wearers habitually drank. Whether you were enjoying yourself or not, in a Bubble dress you were carrying the party with you.

ACCESSORIES: Bare shoulders, expensive jewelry, and a desire to have a really, really good time (or at least look as if you were). The classic 1980s version was worn with sheer black stockings (back seams optional) and dramatic eye makeup; the modern version is worn with bare legs and Botox.

WORN BY: Ivana Trump, Isabella Blow, the social X-rays in *Bonfire of the Vanities*, everyone who was anyone in 1987, and everyone who attended a senior prom in 1988–89.

DESIGNERS: Christian Lacroix, Nathan Jenden.

THE CAFTAN   15

THE CAFTAN, MUU-MUU, OR TENT DRESS, as it is variously known, is a long, loose gown without definition at the waist. The Caftan is usually made of a light fabric, especially silk or cotton, with a V-neck or slit at the neck, and often has decorative embroidery, sequins, or jeweled ornamentation at the sleeve and neck edges and at the hem. The Muu-muu (the name comes from a Hawaiian word meaning "cut off") is a similar shape but is usually made up in fabric patterned with bright flowers, leaves, or other typically Hawaiian motifs. The Tent dress is, oddly, more elegant than its sisters; it is often shorter than the floor-length Caftan or Muu-muu, occasionally asymmetrical as to hem, and often more muted or darker as to color.

The Caftan is one of the best exemplars of more being less being more: more dress means less skin, which means more intrigue and interest in what is (or isn't) underneath. The Caftan wearer revels in the rare conjunction of comfort and allure, as well as the pure sensual pleasure of beautiful fabric against bare skin.

In order to get the full effect of the Caftan, it must be worn intentionally. It's not something thrown on because the day's too hot for "real clothes"—it's an end in itself and must be treated with respect. When you wear a Caftan, move deliberately: make your gestures a little bigger, your strides a little longer, to really indulge in the flow of the fabric around you. You are conducting the dress, not hiding in it.

ACCESSORIES: Untamed hair (flowers optional for the Muu-muu), bare feet or flat jeweled sandals (for the Caftan and Muu-muu—more serious shoes for the Tent dress), paired cuff bracelets; a willingness to lounge, spare hours in the heat of the afternoon, and, if at all possible, a tiled courtyard with a fountain.

RELATED: The Beauxhemian, the Hostess/Patio dress.

WORN BY: Elizabeth Taylor (in her more zaftig periods), Talitha Getty, Diana Vreeland, Marisa Berenson, Rachel Zoe.

DESIGNERS: Christian Dior, Yves Saint Laurent, Cristóbal Balenciaga.

THE CHANEL INGÉNUE

16

ALTHOUGH COCO CHANEL is associated with the little black jersey dress, another iconic House of Chanel dress is the Ingénue. The Chanel Ingénue dress is shortish (above the knee, usually), with short or no sleeves and some youthful detail, such as a round collar, bows, or both. Made in a light, beautiful fabric (silk chiffon and lace are favorites), it is usually a beautiful camellia color: off-white with just a hint of blush pink.

An ingénue is considered a young, naive woman—English borrowed the word *ingénue* from French, where it means "guileless"—but the Chanel Ingénue dress is anything but naive or guileless. (The overlapping set of guileless young women and those who can afford Chanel is not very large, after all.) The word *ingénue* is also used to describe actresses who play young women, and the Chanel Ingénue dress is their natural coloration.

The Chanel Ingénue dress (mostly the brainchild of Chanel designer and space alien Karl Lagerfeld) is a perfectly oxymoronic dress: it conveys that the wearer is a sophisticated innocent. The Ingénue dress manages always to look vestal rather than bridal. You wear this dress to highlight your youth, beauty, and freshness—and your knowledge. To wear the Ingénue dress, you have to know enough to avoid the striving for sophistication that young women often fall prey to, which often entails vampy dresses and harsh makeup. Instead, wearers of the Ingénue dress know that, while it may convey girlishness, it is not worn by girls; it is worn by women.

ACCESSORIES: A body that has not yet entered its fourth decade; soft hair and pink makeup (especially lipstick), girlish shoes and bags, poise.

WORN BY: Blake Lively, Keira Knightley, Rachel Bilson.

DESIGNERS: Coco Chanel, Karl Lagerfield.

COCO CHANEL, WHO WAS NOT exactly the shy and retiring type, claimed to have invented the little black dress. Whether she did or not is disputed (and it is slightly like claiming to have invented vanilla ice cream), but what is not disputed is that her 1926 little black jersey dress was a turning point in women's wardrobes. Chanel changed the black dress into something for everyday, everywhere wear, not just for the more solemn occasions of life.

No fussy ornamentation, no ruffles, no buttons or bows. Just a simple black jersey dress, sleek and to-the-knee—simple enough to be made at home without looking "homemade," broadening its appeal even more.

At its best, the Chanel Jersey Dress (and its many, many knockoffs) is chic and elegant, streamlined and modern: a dress for action. It's no accident that women who mean business—at every level from salesclerk to CEO—often favor Chanel-style jersey dresses. The dress is so effective, in fact, that the main danger is in relying too heavily upon it, turning it from a tool to a crutch. If you wear a different exemplar of the Chanel-style black dress every day for two weeks and have trouble remembering the last time you wore another color found in the eight-Crayola box, you probably need to take a little break from it. The prevalence and preeminence of this dress is the primary motivator behind the perennial "Yes, you can wear color!" articles in women's magazines.

ACCESSORIES: Pearls, heels, a knowing air, the feeling of looking ten pounds thinner.

WORN BY: Even if you can't afford the Chanel versions, you have probably worn a little black dress (in jersey or some other fabric with a little give to it).

DESIGNERS: Coco Chanel, and then everyone else, at every price point.

THE CHEONGSAM

CHEONGSAM (PRONOUNCED "CHONG-SOM"), meaning "long gown," is the Cantonese term for this dress; the Mandarin name is *qipao* or "banner gown," after the Manchu people who wore it and who were divided into administrative units called *qi* or "banners."

The earliest Cheongsam was an A-line gown that fell to just below the knee, with wide three-quarter sleeves. Today the Cheongsam is a tight-fitting sheath dress, often ankle length, with high slits reaching above the knee. It usually has a mandarin collar and an asymmetrical closure (fastened with frogs, ball buttons, or snaps) that runs from the collar across the top of the bust to the armhole and down the right side. Occasionally sleeveless, the Cheongsam more often features short sleeves. Cheongsams are usually made of silk (or silklike) material, frequently brocade or damask, with piping outlining the collar and closure, and can be heavily embroidered. (Oei Hui-lan, the third wife of the Chinese statesman Wellington Koo, claims in one of her autobiographies—yes, she wrote two—that she was personally responsible for the addition of piping to the Cheongsam.)

The Cheongsam was popularized in China by Song Qingling (the wife of Sun Yat-sen), who wore them consistently after 1925. The actress Nancy Kwan, who starred in the 1960 movie *The World of Suzie Wong*, is credited with starting the Western craze for the cheongsam; a picture of Kwan in a formfitting, bright yellow Cheongsam, slit well above the knee, made the cover of *Life* in the fall of 1960.

Like other forms of traditional or quasi-traditional national dress, the Cheongsam can be worn to highlight ethnic connections or heritage; wearing a Cheongsam is a required part of the Miss Asia Pageant, for instance. But for Western women, the Cheongsam is bound up with the idea of exoticism and orientalism—the mysterious East. It can be tricky to pull off a Cheongsam and have it not look like a costume or a souvenir; the safest way is to respect the precarious balance of elegance and sensuality inherent in the dress.

The best reason to wear a Cheongsam is for how good it feels: the beautiful fabric (avoid the tatty rayon brocade), the second-skin tailoring, and the way it demands good posture, a graceful carriage, and holding your head high.

ACCESSORIES: Upswept hair (to show off the high collar), pearl drop earrings, confidence.

DESIGNERS: Suzy Perette, Tom Ford (for Yves Saint Laurent), John Galliano (for Dior), Miuccia Prada, Marc Jacobs (for Louis Vuitton).

THE CHER DRESS is any dress that forces onlookers to hold two simultaneous thoughts: "Wow, I can't believe she wore that!" and "Damn, she looks amazing!"

Cher—said to have been the first woman to expose her navel on television—has been a fashion icon throughout her long career, being one of the first to take up bell-bottoms, tattoos for women, and long, straight hair. She began her creative relationship with designer Bob Mackie on *The Sonny and Cher Comedy Hour* (1971–74), and he also worked with her on *The Cher Show* (1975–76) and *The Sonny and Cher Show* (1976–77). Mackie is the designer we think of when we think of Cher's eye-popping outfits, especially her look for the 1986 Academy Awards: a two-piece "Indian" gown and a two-foot-tall spiky black headdress made of rooster feathers (sometimes called the "spider woman" outfit). Onstage to present the award for Best Supporting Actor, Cher announced that she had obviously received her "Academy booklet on how to dress like a serious actress." In later interviews, Cher has said her Oscar outfit was in reaction to being told that she hadn't received a nomination for her role in the critically acclaimed 1985 film *Mask* because she didn't "dress seriously."

Cher's outfits are costumey, of course, but they're all basically Cher costumes. With each outrageous ensemble, she becomes more herself—whether it's the barely-there shimmer of showgirlesque brilliants she wore to accept the 1988 Best Actress Academy Award for her role in *Moonstruck* or the fishnets-and-thong getup that ensured her 1999 video for "If I Could Turn Back Time" was played on MTV only after 9:00 p.m.

The Cher is what you wear when you need to be yourself, only more so—your own style turned up to eleven, you giving 110 percent, you visible from space. If you like low necklines, your personal Cher dress is millimeters short of a wardrobe malfunction; if you like formfitting skirts, your personal Cher skirt should fit like body paint; if you like loose trapeze shapes, your inner Cher should show up in an actual tent.

ACCESSORIES: Chutzpah, liberal use of the f-word, visible tattoos in places most people don't usually allow to be visible. Feathered headdresses encouraged but optional.

RELATED: The Biohazard, the Stunt Dress, the Swan.

WORN BY: Cher, of course. Nobody else can pull it off!

DESIGNER: Bob Mackie.

THE CLASSIC BRIDE

20

THE CLASSIC BRIDE DRESS, at least the classic bridal dress of the last sixty years or so, is immediately iconic: a formfitting, strapless bodice, usually with boning of some kind, atop a floor-length full skirt.

Although strapless necklines demand serious attention to fit, bridal gowns are one of the few garments the average woman will have extensively altered in her lifetime. And the dream of wearing a big, gorgeous skirt often leads women to balance all that fabric with some bare skin, which is part of the reason this silhouette is so popular—according to Kate Berry, the style director for *Martha Stewart Weddings*, nearly 75 percent of wedding dresses are strapless.

The interest in this dress is in the expression of choice and the working of changes within a fairly rigid framework: fabric in shades of white, cream, ecru, and candlelight; in chiffon, satin, lace, or brocade; bows, sashes, ruffles; appliquéd, embroidered, beaded, or sequined; a train or a bustle, or both; sweetheart neckline or straight band.

The Classic Bride dress can almost be taken as a metaphor for marriage. Here is this institution, this construction of convention, with fairly well-delineated legal, social, and religious obligations, but within it, the two people are making dozens, if not hundreds, of little choices every day that are intended to lead to the effect of greater happiness.

ACCESSORIES: Something old, something new, something borrowed, something blue.

WORN BY: Traditionalists, women who are really fond of their upper arms, any bride whose (nonroyal) wedding is televised.

DESIGNERS: Vera Wang and the rest of the bridal-industrial complex.

THE CLASSIC PARTY DRESS has short sleeves, a short (slightly above the knee) full skirt, and a Peter Pan collar. Made in a soft color (pink, pale blue, pale yellow, white), it doesn't skimp on the ruffles, bows, or nonfunctional buttons. The grown-up (or "stealth") version of the Classic Party Dress keeps the full skirt but ditches the ruffles and bows for a simpler shape in a bright, girly color.

It's obvious that a party dress is intended for parties, especially birthdays, but only grown-ups are so stunted as to think that the party comes first, then the dress. Children understand that the laws of causality don't always work in such pedestrian and mundane ways; if you're already wearing a party dress, why wouldn't a party break out? This is why some six-year-olds want to wear their party dresses every day; if you've noted the strong correlation between a particular type of garment and cake and ice cream, you'd be foolish not to work the odds. Adults think the party demands the dress; kids think the dress creates the party.

It's slightly harder (okay, nearly impossible) for adults to pull off the Classic Party Dress (wearers of Japanese Lolita fashion aside), but many of us fall prey to the same kind of pattern-seeking behavior. The luckiness of our "lucky" dress might not be measured in unexpected cake and ice cream (in fact, we probably hope it isn't), but we probably overremember happy events associated with wearing it, and just by being in a positive frame of mind, expectant of pleasure, we make those events more likely in the future.

ACCESSORIES: White lace-trimmed ankle socks and patent-leather shoes, a hair bow and sausage curls, cake. Giant lollipop allowed only during musical numbers.

RELATED: The Lolita, the Baby Doll.

WORN BY: Shirley Temple, Veruca Salt.

THE COUNTRY MUSIC STAR *22*

FOR A DRESS TO BE WORTHY of a country music star, it has to have at least one of the following: fringe, rhinestones, a saloon color scheme of black and red, a Western yoke, pearl-button snaps, a drinking problem. The Country Music Star dress can be made in denim or satin, can reach to the floor or skyrocket above the knee, and is always, always worn with cowboy boots.

In recent years, some country music stars, especially crossover stars such as Taylor Swift and Carrie Underwood, have left behind the trappings of the Country Music Star dress, at least for the red carpet, looking instead much like celebrities attending any other borrowed-jewelry event—crossover gowns for crossover music. But more traditional stars, such as the irrepressible Dolly Parton (who famously said, "It takes a lot of money to make me look this cheap") and Shania Twain (whose 1998 Grammy dress featured fringed above-the-elbow gloves) continue to wear the trappings of country music stardom both on and off the stage.

The point of the Country Music Star dress is to take the classic tropes of American Western working wear and then to do something equally American with them: glitz them up. A ballgown in silk taffeta with a bandanna print? Country Music Star. A dress with an overall-like bib, in red satin? Country Music Star. Cowboy boots that cost more than a family sedan, worn with a jeweled Stetson and a frayed denim miniskirt? You got it. The message of the Country Music Star dress? It doesn't matter where you came from, it matters where you're going, and you can carry both with you.

ACCESSORIES: A no-good cheating man, a guitar, a gun, a pickup truck, big hair.

OPTIONAL: Keep the price tag on your hat, à la Minnie Pearl.

WORN BY: Much of the hopeful female population of Nashville, Tennessee.

DESIGNERS: Nudie (for inspiration), Ralph Lauren (mostly rhinestoneless interpretations of American clothes).

THE COWGIRL

THE COWGIRL DRESS is an above-the-knee dress, usually in denim, but sometimes in suede or leather, constructed like a typical "Western" shirt: pointed yoke, front patch pockets (sometimes with "sawtooth" double-pointed flaps), mother-of-pearl snap closures, and long sleeves with barrel cuffs. It can feature embroidery (often with rose motifs) or rhinestone embellishment on the yoke, collar, or cuffs. The Cowgirl dress sometimes wants to be the Country Music Star dress when it grows up (and grows fringe).

Jack A. Weil, the founder of Rockmount Ranch Wear, is considered the father of the modern Western shirt—he was the first to popularize and mass-manufacture the snap-button "fancy" variety. The origin of the dress variety is more obscure, but the idea of a feminine, dress-length version of such a pretty and flattering garment had to have occurred to more than one woman buying a Rockmount or H Bar C shirt for her cowboy.

Although Cowgirl as a full-on trend comes and goes, the Cowgirl dress is a classic sportswear style that is never completely out of fashion, especially in the American West. Women who favor the Cowgirl tend to be self-assured, competent, friendly, and competitive; they can, with equal composure, tell you a good joke or to go to hell.

Jack Weil (who himself came from Indiana) said the West was about "romance," and that's what the Cowgirl dress promises. It's not the Disney-princess variety of romance, but the romance of the American frontier: open skies, clear horizons, and endless possibilities, as long as you're willing to buckle down and do the work.

ACCESSORIES: A heavy leather belt with a rodeo-prize buckle, cowboy boots, a Stetson, a pickup truck, a honky-tonk bar, a proficiency at the Texas two-step.

DESIGNERS: Rodeo Ben, Nudie, Ralph Lauren, Dolce and Gabbana.

THE CUPCAKE BRIDE

THE CUPCAKE BRIDE DRESS (sometimes called the Meringue dress) is characterized by one word: *more*. The Cupcake Bride dress has more ruffles, more bows, more fabric, more beads, more lace, more sequins, more train—in short, more anything than you thought it possible to put into one dress.

The cupcake-iest, meringue-iest Cupcake Bride dress of all, of course, is the dress that Lady Diana Spencer wore to marry Prince Charles in 1981. Designed by David and Elizabeth Emanuel, the dress (whose ivory silk taffeta woven especially for Diana was hand-embroidered with mother-of-pearl sequins) included antique Carrickmacross lace that once belonged to Prince Charles's great-grandmother Mary, queen consort of King George V. With a twenty-five-foot train, ten thousand pearls, and sleeves that looked as if they could conceal a Virginia ham, the dress was impractical even for a wedding . . . but despite the James Bond–level security that protected the Emanuels as they designed and constructed the dress, the first knock-off (in polyester satin, not silk taffeta) was available in stores just five hours after the wedding. There were actually two dresses made for the wedding—the designers made a complete backup dress, just in case.

The dress Diana wore was later purchased by Madame Tussaud's for display, and it was sold at auction for more than £84,000 (including a duplicate pair of white lace shoes) in late 2011, to a fashion museum in Chile.

It's understandable that Diana would want to armor herself with as much fabric as possible, to shield herself from the scrutiny of the hundreds of millions of people watching her wedding on television. But wearers of the Cupcake Bride dress today may not be trying to disappear inside acres of taffeta—they may be trying to express externally (in the underused emotional medium of satin bows) the true size of their happiness. And if that results in needing a couple more flower girls to wrangle the train, or if a bridesmaid throws out her back adjusting a bustle, who can really begrudge those small sacrifices in the service of joy?

ACCESSORIES: A prince (charm optional), and a strong back to carry the weight of all that fabric.

WORN BY: Princess Diana.

THE DEBUTANTE

THE DEBUTANTE DRESS is a long formal dress, often with a sweetheart or off-the-shoulder neckline. It is usually white, although occasionally pale pastel colors are used.

The word *débutante* dates from the early 1800s, when Queen Charlotte (wife of King George III) began the tradition of presenting young aristocratic women at court. What could be worn at these occasions became strictly regulated by the Lord Chamberlain's office, with full court dress consisting of

> low bodice, short sleeves, and train to dress not less than three yards in length from the shoulders. Whether the train is cut round or square is a matter of inclination or fashion. The width at the end should be 54 inches. It is also imperative that a presentation dress should be white, if the person presented be an unmarried lady; and it is also the fashion for married ladies to wear white on their presentation unless their age rendered their doing so unsuitable. The white dresses worn by either débutante or married ladies may be trimmed with either colored or white flowers according to individual taste.

Feathers—a "court plume"—were also required, "worn so they can be clearly seen on approaching the presence" (i.e., the queen), with married women wearing three white feathers and unmarried women two. (And before you ask, no, this is not the origin of "a feather in one's cap"—that phrase dates back at least a hundred years earlier, and a feather in the cap was also the traditional sign of a fool.)

Although a very small percentage of North American women actually make a formal debut these days, either at court or at cotillion balls, the Debutante dress is often worn for formal occasions where emphasizing one's youth, innocence, social importance, or connection to old money is desirable. (The custom of the *quinceañera*, a party given for a fifteen-year-old girl to celebrate her transition from girlhood to womanhood, is popular in Spanish-speaking countries in Latin America and among American Latinos, and can also include a white dress.)

ACCESSORIES: Long white gloves, a tasteful corsage, the handsome scion of a moneyed New York family, Daddy.

WORN BY: Brenda Frazier, Barbara Hutton, Jacqueline Bouvier, Gloria Vanderbilt.

THE DEPRESSION HOUSEWIFE

26

THE DEPRESSION HOUSEWIFE DRESS is a simple cotton housedress, usually fastening up the front with buttons or a zipper, with large patch or side-seam pockets, and often a collar. Made in busy cotton prints (so as not to show dirt or stains) and occasionally from printed flour or feed sacks, these dresses are easy to wash and easy to wear.

Despite their owners' straitened circumstances, real Depression-era housedresses were often made in cheery prints. Popular prints included florals, plaids, stripes, and "conversation" prints (so-called because they were supposed to elicit comments): teeny-tiny horseshoes, weathervanes, acorns, and so on. Depression-era housedresses used buttons, not the newfangled (and expensive) "zip fasteners."

Although most housework these days is done (and many spells of depression are spent) in sweatpants and a T-shirt, the Depression Housewife dress is still a perfect choice for less-than-ideal situations. It's comfortable and practical, and it lends an air of can-do competence to even the most difficult conditions. It says that even when circumstances are grim, you can at least be clean and cheerful.

ACCESSORIES: Low oxford shoes, a dime tied in a handkerchief, a slightly worried expression.

WORN BY: Few celebrities are photographed in the Depression Housewife: the celebrities of the time were tricked out in satin and marabou for escapism's sake, while modern lovers of vintage prefer the dressier rayon versions or the 1950s June Cleaver. One notable screen version is worn by Jessica Lange in the 1981 movie version of *The Postman Always Rings Twice.*

DESIGNERS INSPIRED BY THE DEPRESSION HOUSEWIFE DRESS (AT MUCH HIGHER PRICES): Prada, Diane von Furstenberg.

THE DIRNDL 27

ACCORDING TO THE AUSTRIAN Tourist Office (not exactly an unbiased source), no less an authority than designer Vivienne Westwood said that "there would be no ugliness in the world if every woman wore a dirndl." Eradicating ugliness is a tall order for a dress, but there is something both *heimisch* and full of *gemütlichkeit* about the full skirt, tight bodice, white blouse, and apron of the classic dirndl. (Traditional Bavarian clothing, including dirndls and lederhosen, is sometimes lumped together under the heading of *tracht*.)

Oktoberfest is, of course, the classic time to wear a Dirndl (or the more costumey Wench variant), but a classic Dirndl deserves to be worn more than a few weeks out of the year. The Dirndl manages to be simultaneously practical and attractive. It's close-fitting, but the deep armholes and free skirt allow for easy movement. It's traditional, but it allows for modern interpretations (there are fashion-forward versions of the Dirndl in leather, lamé, and even Sari silks). As with many forms of national or ethnic dress, it can be tricky for outsiders to wear the Dirndl without looking like you're on your theme-park cigarette break, but the Dirndl might be worth taking that risk. Choose a dark fabric without embroidery, pair it with a simple blouse and low heels, and leave the apron at home, topping it with a short jacket instead, and you have an updated traditional ensemble that you could wear nearly anywhere.

RELATED: The Dorothy, the Wench.

WORN BY: Julie Andrews (in *The Sound of Music*, costumes designed by Dorothy Jeakins), Dita von Teese, Kim Kardashian (in the Wench version, of course).

DESIGNERS: Munich designer Lola Paltinger.

28

THE DISNEY DRESS is familiar to anyone who has ever seen an animated movie: it has a tight, low-cut bodice with a pointed basque (the part that extends below the waist), short puffed or off-the-shoulder sleeves, and a long, full skirt. The bodice and skirt can be of different materials, and the dress is sometimes obtained by unconventional means (wishes, magic, pen and ink).

The Disney dress is worn by three demographics: actual cartoon characters, young girls playing dress-up, and women playing dress-up (that is, brides). Wearing a Disney dress is an acknowledgment that we all have an innate wish for happily-ever-after, whether it comes in a Prince Charming–shaped package or not. The promise of the Disney dress is that the combination of a kind heart, a tendency to burst into song, and just a little bit of bravery at the right time should lead to everything working out just fine (and, preferably, ending in a clinch set to strings and birdsong).

Of course, we never actually see the promised happily-ever-after of the Disney dress; there are no epilogues, no bluebirds interviewed for a "the making of" show. It's entirely possible that those full skirts are cut up to make curtains for the palace, or that a tight bodice doesn't show so well twenty years down the road. But none of that can (or should) impede the wearing of a Disney dress.

ACCESSORIES: Bluebirds and helpful forest animals, wicked stepmothers, kindness, singing.

WORN BY: Snow White, Sleeping Beauty, Cinderella, Belle.

> Dorothy had only one other dress, but that happened to be clean and was hanging on a peg beside her bed. It was gingham, with checks of white and blue; and although the blue was somewhat faded with many washings, it was still a pretty frock.
>
> —L. Frank Baum, *The Wonderful Wizard of Oz*

THE DOROTHY DRESS is any dress in which you find yourself having an unexpected adventure. In many adventure stories, a great deal of attention is paid to outfitting yourself for the journey. You have to gather armor and weapons and provisions, heavy wool traveling cloaks, garments with handy pockets, new boots. Not so for Dorothy. She has one other dress, and it's clean and pretty enough, so that is what she will wear to set out for the Emerald City.

In the original novel, Dorothy's gingham dress marks her as a friendly sorceress to the Munchkins—a sorceress because in Oz only witches and sorceresses wear white, and friendly because she is also wearing blue, the color of the Munchkins.

Although Dorothy has no warning before the cyclone carries her off to Oz (and is an orphan in rural Kansas with little say over what she wears, besides), we are luckier. When we choose a new dress, do we think, "What if I had to set off on an adventure in this?" If not, maybe we should.

(In an interesting aside, the frock coat worn by the actor Frank Morgan, who played the Wizard in the 1939 film, had been purchased in a secondhand store . . . and turned out to have L. Frank Baum's name stitched inside. The character was wearing his inventor's clothes.)

ACCESSORIES: A little basket, a little dog, a plucky can-do spirit, good friends and traveling companions met along the road, and magical shoes (in the book they were silver, but in the movie, of course, they were ruby slippers).

WORN BY: Dorothy.

DESIGNER: The 1939 movie costumes were designed by Adrian.

DRESS FOR SUCCESS was the title of John T. Molloy's 1975 book about "wardrobe engineering" for the practice of "power dressing," described by Molloy as dressing to look powerful and competent. *Dress for Success* only covered wardrobe engineering for men, however, so Molloy published a follow-up in 1977, *The Women's Dress for Success Book*.

In the early 1970s, while researching his book for women, Molloy tested 646 different dress styles, asking business executives which dresses signaled competence and other executive qualities in the wearer. His (not very scientific) findings were that dresses tested poorly when compared with skirted suits or dresses worn with jackets, except for the role of "executive wife" (again, this was the 1970s). Molloy advocated dark conservative suits for both sexes (with allowable flashes of color in brooches, ties, and pocket squares), but because dark conservative suits are both expensive and dull, women persisted in wearing dresses to the office.

If you must wear a dress, Molloy says, you should wear dresses that look expensive, are conservatively tailored, and are navy, medium blue, tan, beige, grayish brown, or dark brown. (Unsurprisingly, rust-colored dresses worked well in the 1970s, but not so well today.) Dressing for success is, in a word, boring.

Today, the *Dress for Success* look is considered dated, but it still persists in more rigid and hierarchical industries. Wearing it indicates conservatism and willingness to follow the rules—not the qualities touted as those of high-performing executives in most business books today—and is more likely to mark you as middle management than as CEO material.

ACCESSORIES: Rolodex, pantyhose, athletic shoes (worn on commute).

NOT WORN BY: Some of the most successful women in business, such as Marissa Mayer (of Yahoo!), Indra Nooyi (of Pepsi), Arianna Huffington (of the *Huffington Post*).

THE DURO DRESS, a Kimono-like silk dress with wide sleeves and a high waist, is accentuated at the waist, sleeves, and hem with wide contrasting bands. Designed by Nigerian-born London-based lawyer-turned-designer Duro Olowu, the original Duro dress was voted the dress of the year in 2005 by both British and American *Vogue*. Olowu himself also won the 2005 Best New Designer of the Year award from the British Fashion Council.

The Duro dress is, at heart, a dress about joy. It's impossible to be glum or miserable surrounded by so much vibrant color and so many exuberant patterns. Not only is it physically easy to wear because of its forgiving shape and soft, flowing fabric, it's emotionally easy to wear, too. Because the colors and patterns are meshed together in one garment, there's none of the self-doubt or lack of confidence that can strike the wearer who assembles her own collage. The Duro is a designer dress, after all—it's supposed to look the way it does.

Wearers of the Duro dress end up self-confident, open, and happy, whether or not they started out that way when they put it on in the morning.

ACCESSORIES: Platform shoes or knee-high boots, a statement necklace, natural, simple hair, a love for color and pattern.

WORN BY: Michelle Obama, Uma Thurman, Iman.

THE DYNASTY

THE DYNASTY DRESS originated on the nighttime television soap of the same name, which ran on ABC from 1981 to 1989. Following the oil-rich Carrington family of Denver, the show included a number of preposterous and melodramatic events, including arson, comas, royal weddings, miscarriages, massacres, murder trials, plastic surgery, amnesia, heart transplants, and kidnapping.

But the real drama of the show was in the clothes—the jewel-toned, sequined and beaded, strong-shouldered, dramatic gowns (and hats and veils and stoles and turbans) worn by the female leads, especially by Joan Collins as the scheming Alexis. Costume designer Nolan Miller, who once designed costumes for Joan Crawford, was given an enormous budget for the show ($25,000 an episode) and was instructed that no main character should wear the same outfit twice—which meant that thirty-five to forty ensembles were designed and created every week. Miller became famous for his work on *Dynasty*, to the point where he received more than a hundred fan letters a week in 1984. (He also won an Emmy for his work on the show that year.)

Although the Dynasty dress seems more camp than chic today, it's still a powerful and magnetic dress—and perfect for a busy day of double-crosses, catfights, and perjury.

ACCESSORIES: A hat (the hat's flamboyance nicely correlated with the wearer's degree of bitchiness), extremely large and vulgar jewelry, dramatic makeup, elaborately complicated oil-related paperwork, and a cloud of Forever Krystle perfume.

WORN BY: Joan Collins (as Alexis), Linda Evans (as Krystle), and Diahann Carroll (as Dominique Deveraux).

DESIGNERS: Nolan Miller, Francesco Scognamiglio.

THE FACE DRESS is usually a simple shape, like a shift or a trapeze, with a large representation of a human face printed or woven (or, occasionally, appliquéd) on it. Wearers of the Face know that human beings—even newborns—prefer to look at things that resemble faces, and huge, colorful faces are even better. So Face dresses are huge attention getters, doubly so if the face is a famous one—Marilyn Monroe, Andy Warhol, Elvis—or if the eyes and mouth of the face are strategically placed to be provocative.

When you wear a face dress, you have to keep everything else simple—shoes, hair, and your own face, too; otherwise you start to look like a two-headed monster. The Face dress is young and playful, but it does have one downside—while you're wearing it you give up the option of saying, "Hey buddy, my eyes are *up here*."

ACCESSORIES: At most, an armful of bangle bracelets.

WORN BY: It's difficult to find celebrities in the Face dress; they prefer not to have another fabulous face competing so closely with their own.

DESIGNERS: Yves Saint Laurent, Stephen Sprouse, Franco Moschino, Kansai Yamamoto, Jean-Charles de Castelbajac, Lisa Perry.

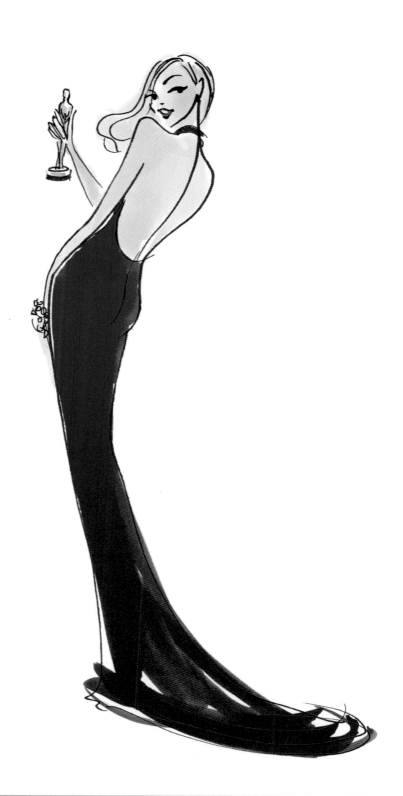

THE FIRST OSCAR

OF ALL THE HIGH-STAKES DRESSES in the world, the dress worn upon first being nominated for an Academy Award may be the highest. Here are the adjectives you want associated with your first Oscar dress: *old-Hollywood, elegant, gorgeous.* Here are the ones you do not: *edgy, fashion-forward, weird.* The First Oscar dress, then, is old-Hollywood, elegant, and gorgeous: a halter or strapless neckline, a long, formfitting skirt (usually with a fishtail hem or slight train), and a conservative color (red, in this scenario, counts as conservative).

The days when the Academy Awards ceremony was a bunch of slightly drunk friends getting together for a combination of mutual back-patting and celebrity roasting are long over (if, in fact, that ever happened). Now the Oscars are just part of the job, and the occasion has to be prepared for accordingly. Think of it as an evening off-site with a strict dress code and a lot of very picky clients. The First Oscar dress is probably the most glamorous example of the perennial business-fashion advice that you should "dress for the job you want, not the job you have." The job wanted here is "Academy Award–winning actress," and although the votes have all been counted before you step out on the red carpet in your Oscar-worthy gown, dressing the part can only help—if just to make sure your win is counted as a foregone conclusion instead of a fluke.

ACCESSORIES: As many diamonds as you can borrow, shoes that could get their own half-hour special on E!, and, ideally, a romantic coupling of your name with that of the male lead from the nominated movie.

RELATED: The Siren, the Women.

WORN BY: Renée Zellweger, Rooney Mara, Jennifer Lawrence, Marion Cotillard.

DESIGNERS: Carolina Herrera (for Zellweger), Givenchy (for Mara), Francisco Costa for Calvin Klein (for Lawrence), Jean Paul Gaultier (for Cotillard).

THE FLAMENCO DRESS (in Spanish, *traje de flamenca*) originated in the dress of the Roma people in Andalusia, and is now considered a typically Andalusian garment. Often a *traje de lunares*, or polka-dot dress, it typically is ankle length or longer, with copious ruffles on both the skirt and the sleeves. (Some writers have said that the ruffles of the Flamenco dress represent the pink-edged petals of a carnation.) Although the general shape remains the same, dress designers show new fashions in Flamenco every year, at the Salón Internacional de la Moda Flamenca.

The most important thing in flamenco performance is what's called *duende*—that eerie sadness, the dark sounds that raise the hair on the back of your neck. The poet Federico García Lorca said that *duende* needs "the trembling of the moment and then a long silence." The Flamenco dress may look cheerful with all those ruffles, but the wearer should bear some heavy weight on the soul, a darkness of the heart, a shadow of loss. Like the flamenco dancer, the wearer of the Flamenco dress should be able to transmit waves of feeling to onlookers without seeming to expend any special effort to do so.

ACCESSORIES: The Flamenco dress is worn with high-heeled laced oxfords, an optional black lace mantilla or flowers in the hair, and an air of barely controlled passion.

WORN BY: You haven't truly seen a Flamenco dress until you see one worn by a true flamenco artist, such as Carmen Amaya or Soledad Barrio.

DESIGNERS: Tom Ford, John Galliano, Yves Saint Laurent—but really, anytime a designer puts a ruffle (or two, or three) on a dress, the fashion press cries, "Flamenco!"

THE FLAPPER   36

THE ICONIC FLAPPER DRESS is red, fringed, spaghetti-strapped, and above the knee. (Actual flapper dresses were usually just below the knee but seemed scandalously short compared to the ankle-grazing dresses of the period.)

The message of the Flapper has been diluted in the ninety-some years since it first made its appearance: it started as the dress of sexual freedom but is now a quaint cliché of American sartorial history, like Rosie the Riveter.

The Flapper was sometimes called La Garçonne (from the French for "boy," but with a feminine suffix, meaning something like the English "tomboy"), after a 1922 French novel of the same name by Victor Margueritte. In it, a young woman learns that her fiancé is cheating on her, and she decides to live life in the same way, with multiple sexual partners. The claim of equal sexual freedom for women made by the flapper is ironically offset by the dress's insistence on a boyish silhouette. To wear the Flapper dress requires a straight up-and-down figure with no hint of bosom or hips—pure youthful androgyny, a reaction to the imposingly mature bustle-and-bust S-curves of the prior era.

ACCESSORIES: A cigarette holder, a long strand of pearls, bobbed hair, a cloche hat or headband, a feather boa, rolled stockings, T-strap shoes, bathtub gin, and the Charleston.

WORN BY: Daisy Buchanan, Clara Bow, Louise Brooks, Coco Chanel, girls in John Held Jr. cartoons, countless costume-party attendees.

DESIGNERS: Ralph Lauren, Marc Jacobs, Oscar de la Renta.

THE FLASHDANCE

37

THE FLASHDANCE IS ANY SLOUCHY, off-the-shoulder dress, usually worn well above the knee. Ideally, it looks like a distressed gray sweatshirt, although in practice, for most figures, it is not so easy to turn any old sweatshirt into a flattering dress. The Flashdance dress is all about the *sprezzatura* of the dancer—that art of making difficult things look graceful. The Flashdance myth goes something like this: you may have just rehearsed for four grueling hours, but you can walk out of the practice studio with a scissored-up sweatshirt tossed over your leotard and look better than if you had spent the whole day primping in front of the mirror.

The 1983 movie *Flashdance* was the start of the trend—it starred Jennifer Beals as a welder with classical-dance aspirations. Michael Kaplan was the costume designer for the movie (and he won a best-costume award from the British Academy of Film and Television Arts that same year for his work on *Blade Runner*), but according to later interviews with Beals, after she wore a ripped-neck sweatshirt to one of her auditions, a version of it became part of her costume.

The Flashdance dress is dancer chic with a bit more edge; it's not the pretty-pretty wrap sweater and pink tights of the typical bunhead. The Flashdance and the tutu don't speak to each another.

ACCESSORIES: Unless you're in costume, avoid wearing the Flashdance dress as the foundation of an amalgamation of 1980s references—limit yourself to one only from the set of legwarmers, headbands, rubber shoes or bracelets, and neon jewelry.

WORN BY: Jennifer Beals (in the movie), early Madonna, early Madonna wannabes.

DESIGNERS: Domenico Dolce and Stefano Gabbana (for their D&G line, back in 2002) and Michael Kors are among the designers who have sent Flashdancesque looks down the runway.

THE FLOWER CHILD BRIDE

38

THE FLOWER CHILD BRIDE DRESS is usually high-waisted and ankle length, and often ruffled. Made in soft, more casual fabrics (especially cotton lawn, dotted swiss, and eyelet), it is much less formal than the traditional silk and satin wedding gown. Ivory, off-white, blush pink, primrose yellow, and pale blue are all possible colors, in addition to pure white, and embellishment tends to be of the cross-stitched, cotton eyelet, or crocheted variety, instead of beading, sequins, or fancy embroidery.

The idea of the Flower Child Bride dress is that even though marriage is a signal transition point to adulthood, it's possible to enter it in a youthful spirit, to delay the advent of matronhood by holding tight to girlishness. The hope is to try to ward off the boring, stuffy accoutrements of grown-up marriage (high heels, blenders, mortgages) by replacing the boring, stuffy accoutrements of traditional weddings: eyelet instead of lace, in the garden rather than at the altar, a potluck instead of a banquet, a guy with a guitar instead of a wedding band.

ACCESSORIES: The great outdoors, a wreath of flowers in the hair, bare feet, and a bouquet of daisies. Flower Child grooms often wear tunic-type shirts, dashikis, or smocks.

RELATED: The Beauxhemian.

WORN BY (AND DESIGNED BY): Julianne Moore wore a lilac Prada dress for her 2003 wedding to director Bart Freundlich and Tori Spelling wore an eyelet Dolce & Gabbana dress (one of two different Dolce & Gabbana dresses chosen for the event) for her wedding to Dean McDermott in 2006. Milla Jovovich wore a long white Temperley column dress for her 2009 wedding to director Paul W. S. Anderson but then switched for the reception to a hippie-style minidress of her own design, created with vintage lace fabric that originally had been commissioned by Coco Chanel.

THE FORTUNY   **39**

MARIANO FORTUNY (1871–1949, in full Mariano Fortuny y Madrazo) had artistic beginnings. He was the son of the Spanish painter Mariano Fortuny y Marsal and was informally tutored in Paris by the sculptor Auguste Rodin. Fortuny began his career as a set designer for opera—he was fascinated by Wagner—and started experimenting with textiles in the late 1890s. Inspired by the rich Renaissance colors and Byzantine mosaics of Venice, where he had made his home, as well as by classical models, he began creating vegetable-dyed gowns and cloaks. The Fortuny dress is a classically inspired column of pleated silk, sleeveless or with dolman sleeves; early versions tied at the waist with a silk cord. The pleats are given weight with tiny Murano glass beads. Fortuny patented the method for pleating the fabric in 1909, one of more than twenty textile-related patents he filed in his lifetime.

The Fortuny is one of the notable dresses of literature, mentioned more than a dozen times in Proust's *Remembrance of Things Past*:

> Of all the outdoor and indoor gowns that Mme. de Guermantes wore, those which seemed most to respond to a definite intention, to be endowed with a special significance, were the garments made by Fortuny from old Venetian models. Is it their historical character, is it rather the fact that each one of them is unique that gives them so special a significance that the pose of the woman who is wearing one while she waits for you to appear or while she talks to you assumes an exceptional importance, as though the costume had been the fruit of a long deliberation and your conversation was detached from the current of everyday life like a scene in a novel?

The original Fortuny dresses were considered too informal and unstructured to be worn on the street—they were for home wear only, as "tea gowns." And to wear a Fortuny dress today is still to be a secret gem, a hidden palazzo in Venice, a muse. Like the pleating process itself, which has never been fully duplicated, any woman in a Fortuny dress is unique.

ACCESSORIES: Simple sandals, a Fortuny "Knossos" scarf (a large piece of silk printed with geometric designs) in a contrasting color, and the air of being a timeless work of art.

WORN BY: Isadora Duncan, Peggy Guggenheim, Martha Graham, Queen Marie of Romania.

DESIGNERS INSPIRED BY FORTUNY: Mary McFadden, Madame Grès, Issey Miyake, Stella McCartney, and (by their own admission) Mary-Kate and Ashley Olsen.

THE GARDEN PARTY DRESS used to be as well regulated as the evening gown: there were definite rules, and breaking them was a social sin (so much so that the "I have nothing to wear to the garden party!" seems to be a trope of Edwardian popular fiction). An etiquette manual from the early 1920s states, "Women always dress for a garden party in their lightest flower-festooned hats and delicate chiffons, georgettes, and organdies, and carry their fluffiest sunshades and wear their whitest gloves," and Emily Post herself said, "If you have a very elaborate summer dress, this [a garden party] is the only time you can wear it!"

As one late Victorian etiquette book put it, the perfect garden party is "a green lawn, a few trees, a fine day and something to eat"; the perfect Garden Party dress is not very much more complicated. The ideal Garden Party dress is more of a concept than a category: it combines a lightweight gorgeous fabric with a simple silhouette, and takes advantage of the outdoor setting to indulge in pretty colors or (as with the Bouquet dress) floral prints or appliqués.

The closest thing we have to the garden party these days is the outdoor summer wedding, and the rules for Garden Party dresses apply there, too. A pale pink cotton lawn dress with a darker pink shawl, a full-skirted dress with a border print of yellow roses, or a Nile green column dress are all more suitable than the mélange of gray businessy dresses or little black evening dresses that look so out of place on the lawn in the sunshine.

ACCESSORIES: In addition to the sunshade or parasol, the Garden Party dress should be worn with light shoes (flats or wedges are best if you suspect you may otherwise aerate the lawn with each step). Silk shawls or pale cardigans are useful as the evening draws on, but flower-trimmed hats and white gloves are strictly optional.

RELATED: The Bouquet dress, the Classic Party dress.

WORN BY: Attendees at fund-raising garden parties (such as those held by the Museum of Modern Art or the Frick Collection) and the luncheon of the Women's Committee of the Central Park Conservancy.

DESIGNERS: Oscar de la Renta, Carolina Herrera.

THE GRECIAN GOWN

41

THE ANCIENT GREEKS wore very simple clothes, since inventing democracy and philosophy and the resulting arguing meant that they had little time to devote to their wardrobes. Most Greeks wore a chiton, a simple wool or linen tunic made of two rectangles and belted at the waist. Women's chitons were usually ankle length and often worn in the Doric style (called a *peplos*), where the top part was folded over and pinned at the shoulder, with the excess fabric hanging to the waist. (The pins were handy for other things—according to Herodotus, the Doric style was outlawed in Athens after women killed a returning soldier with the pins from their dresses.) The Ionic style lacked the folded top (and so revealed more of the body), and was usually belted with a thin cord worn higher than the natural waist.

Classical dress styles had their most intense revival in postrevolutionary France. Alexandre Dumas described them in his novel *The Whites and the Blues*:

> She was called the meiveilleuse. She borrowed her raiment, not from a new fashion like the *incoyable*, but from antiquity, from the Greek and Corinthian draperies of the Phrynes and the Aspasias. Tunic, peplum, and mantle, all were cut after the fashion of antiquity. The less a woman had on to conceal her nakedness the more elegant she was. The true meiveilleuse, or merveilleuses—for that of course was the real word—had bare arms and legs, the tunic, modeled after that of Diana, was often separated at the side, with nothing more than a cameo to catch the two parts together above the knee.

(The letter *r* was left out of *merveilleuse* and *incroyable* because it was the letter of the French Revolution.)

The most famous modern incarnation of the Greek gown is that of Madame Grès, who in the 1930s made white sleeveless matte silk jersey dresses that fell in classical pleats to the floor. The classical dress is always popular because it borrows against our reverence for the art and culture of the ancients, as well as the aesthetic preference we extend to antique statuary (no matter how battered). The combination of flowing drapery and the human body has been known to be effective for thousands of years and has yet to lose any of its power.

ACCESSORIES: Bands or braids in the hair (or short curls), flat sandals, gold jewelry, and (if you can manage it) a calm half smile.

RELATED: The Fortuny.

WORN BY: Kate Middleton, Charlize Theron, Anne Hathaway.

DESIGNERS: Fortuny, Madame Grès, Vionnet, Marchesa, Elie Saab, Reem Acra.

THE GUINEVERE IS RARELY SEEN on the street these days—its natural home is the Renaissance Faire or the fairy-tale movie (and occasionally the Renaissance Faire bride), but it remains iconic. The Guinevere is floor length, with a slight train, and long tight or belled sleeves ending in points that extend over the hands. The Guinevere has a low-necked or off-the-shoulder bodice that fits tightly through the hips, flaring out into a full skirt. It may be embroidered or brocaded, and is belted (or, to use the right word, girdled) with a cord or chain, often gilt.

The Guinevere, a fairy-tale dress, is about the problem of fairy tales: the happily ever after. The Guinevere looks lovely, romantic, and soft-focus, and it is well-nigh impossible to do a damn thing in it. You can't walk (the long chain belt and the skirt get in the way), you can't lift, carry, or hold anything (the too-tight bodice and the drippy sleeves make that impossible), and the tight fit through the hips means you can't sit down comfortably (you can half recline). The Guinevere is a metaphor, really: it highlights that the princess is the object, not the subject, of the story.

ACCESSORIES: A window with a view (for you to stand next to), a golden circlet, a hint of cleavage, and very, very, very long hair. Dragons, kings, knights, and other heroes are optional.

RELATED: The Disney.

WORN BY: Guinevere (duh), Buttercup in *The Princess Bride*, the Lady of Shalott. Because of the aforementioned logistical problems involved in wearing it, very few modern women attempt it.

THE GYPSY

THE GYPSY DRESS OR COSTUME is usually a combination of a low-cut, off-the-shoulder bodice and a long, full, tiered skirt. Fringed shawls, gold jewelry (especially large earrings and necklaces of coins), long curly dark hair, and bare feet are optional.

The Gypsy dress signifies freedom, independence, and a strong-willed (if not outright defiant) personality. The Gypsy of popular culture is high-spirited, exotic, alluring, and clever, as well as earthy and physical—and the color, movement, sound, and shape of the Gypsy dress all work together to reinforce the impression of liveliness and verve. Laughing is almost obligatory while wearing a Gypsy dress, and will serve to gather attention in almost any situation.

It's important to note that the Gypsy dress is largely a construction of *gadje*, or outsiders, and bears little resemblance to the customary dress of many modern Romany cultures—for instance, some Roma in Finland wear loose black dresses that completely cover the arms and legs, with very full skirts, while some Roma in Albania prefer rose-patterned dresses and gold embroidery; Chilean Xoraxane Rom may also wear long colorful skirts, and married women may tie a *dikló*, or handkerchief, over their hair.

RELATED: The Beauxhemian.

DESIGNERS: Christian Dior, Yves Saint Laurent.

A WOMAN IN A KNEE-LENGTH, earth-tone A-line knit dress, with long sleeves and a drapey cowl neckline, worn with a narrow belt, strides confidently through advertisement after advertisement of the 1970s. Despite a slight tendency to itchiness (due to overreliance on artificial fibers) and a distressing lack of pockets, this silhouette was extremely popular, and it was often topped off with a head neatly coiffed in the hairstyle of the decade, the Hamill.

Figure skater Dorothy Hamill, who won a gold medal in the 1976 Winter Olympics in Innsbruck, popularized the "wedge" haircut. The dancer and choreographer Twyla Tharp had a Vidal Sassoon–scissored version, but Hamill's was cut by celebrity hairstylist Yusuke Suga, who was then at Bergdorf Goodman in New York. (Hamill said it had taken her two years to get the appointment with Mr. Suga.) A *New York Times* article in 1976 reported on the sweeping fad, saying "most women pronounce it 'cute,' 'comfortable,' 'easy to manage.' 'It moves so well,' they say, shaking their heads to show what they mean."

Like the haircut, the Hamill dress is all about ease of movement and swinginess. Warm, cozy, and comfortable, the dress just moves well—important in an era where women were expected to do more and more but were accommodated less and less.

ACCESSORIES: A tooled leather saddlebag handbag and stacked-heel shoes, a smile and an energetic stride, unflappability in the wake of the surprisingly saccharine catcalls of TV-commercial construction workers.

WORN BY: Every Gen-Xer's mother; women who wore Charlie perfume; the heads of all the PTAs for an entire decade.

DESIGNERS: Anne Klein, Bill Blass, John Kloss (for slightly racier versions).

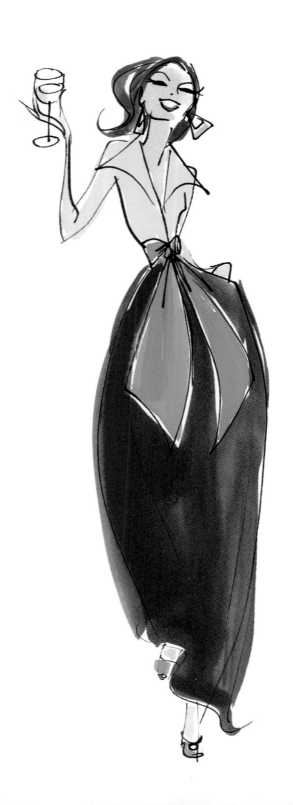

THE HOSTESS/PATIO DRESS

THE CLASSIC 1970S HOSTESS/PATIO DRESS is long—ankle or even floor length. It's bright—orange, pink, green, or combinations thereof, and the wilder the combination, the better. It usually has long sleeves and is either loose, like a Caftan, or tied at the waist with a sash. And it's flowy, whether in natural or (more likely) artificial fibers. It's not a real Hostess/Patio dress unless there is a significant risk of an unfortunate interaction between the dress and a lit tea light.

The hostess is responsible for setting the mood of the party, and the Hostess/Patio dress is responsible for setting the mood of the hostess. It should be festive, but not so fancy that you can't make a pitcher of drinks or bend over the stove in it; it should be comfortable enough for a long night, but not look like a long nightgown. It should survive being bunched up and used as an emergency potholder, but under no circumstances should it actually match your potholders. The perfect Hostess/Patio dress is one that doesn't show spills, excess cleavage, or boredom (when the party is almost over and you want those last straggling guests to just *go home already*).

ACCESSORIES: Flat slippers or sandals (or bare feet), fun earrings, a strengthening drink before the first guest arrives, a plate of pigs-in-blankets, and (back in the 1970s) a slight blush due to an indecent yet flattering proposal from someone else's husband.

RELATED: The Caftan, the Beauxhemian.

DESIGNERS: Emilio Pucci.

THE HUIPIL (pronounced "we-PEEL") is a lightweight cotton dress with colorful embroidery across the front, shoulders, and hem. It usually falls to just below the knee and is constructed of two or three panels that are joined together with ribbons or edge stitching. (Shorter versions, worn as blouses, are also called *huipils*.)

The embroidered Huipil is known throughout Mexico and Central America, and Huipils with more complex designs and more colorful embroidery convey more status on the wearer. Machine-embroidered Huipils are less valuable but come in more varieties, which are named for their style of embroidery, including the *relleno* (filled), *sombreado* (outlined), *calado* (fretwork), and *rejillado* (netting). Some communities sew and embroider Huipils for sale to tourists, which is how they became popular with North Americans. The Internet has made it possible to buy extremely beautiful handmade Huipils more directly from the skilled artisans who make them, and they've become items of fascination to textile collectors, much like antique Kimonos or handmade European lace.

The Anglo wearer of the Huipil dress is usually attracted to the folkloric nature of the embroidery and the ease of wear.

ACCESSORIES: Flat sandals and a hat, often a bathing suit underneath, and occasionally with the memories of a pleasant vacation.

RELATED: The Caftan, the Beauxhemian.

DESIGNERS INSPIRED BY THE HUIPIL: Anna Sui, Isabel Marant.

THE INVISIBLE DRESS

THE INVISIBLE DRESS IS, unsurprisingly, difficult to describe. It's not actually invisible, either in the Harry Potter sense (although metamaterials science is advancing every day) or in the Emperor's New Clothes sense. Rather, the invisible dress is invisible as a direct result of the wearer's character.

The Invisible Dress may not be invisible to the wearer—she may have put much thought and effort into it—but it disappears from everyone else's view, overshadowed by pure personality. If you've ever spent an hour hanging on someone's every word but ten minutes later can't remember what she was wearing, she was wearing an Invisible Dress.

Unfortunately, though, you can't deliberately set out to make your dress into an Invisible Dress; it's a phenomenon that can only happen inadvertently. If you try to convert an unfortunate dress into an Invisible Dress by cracking too many jokes and attempting to be the life of the party, you end up just being an annoying person in an unfortunate dress.

Occasionally an Invisible Dress is worn by someone who is invisible all the way through—someone who takes up so little space that her entire person disappears, not just the dress. These are the people who are always getting pushed to the back of the line, are overlooked by greeters and seaters, and who hear the phrase "Oh, sorry, didn't see you there" dozens of times a day.

ACCESSORIES: A memorable laugh, sparkling wit, a store of fascinating anecdotes that never veer into vulgar name-dropping, irrepressible personal charm, and frequent touches to conversational partners' forearms.

RELATED: The Invisible Dress is the antithesis of the Addicted to Love and the Stunt dress.

DESIGNERS: Many designers have made versions of the Invisible Dress, but, of course, nobody remembers them.

THE IS-IT-A-SHIRT?

THE IS-IT-A-SHIRT? DRESS is one that we all recognize when we see it, but opinions of its shirtiness differ wildly (especially between mothers and daughters). The purpose of the Is-It-a-Shirt? is to provoke outrage from parents, stares from passersby, and the question that gives the dress its name: "Is that a shirt?"

The salient feature of this dress is its length, or lack of it. If the hem extends past your fingertips when you're standing with your arms at your side, then it's not an Is-It-a-Shirt?—it's just a Shirtdress. This dress should stop a good four or so inches before your fingertips, or just below the curve of your rear, whichever is higher. It's permissible to belt an Is-It-a-Shirt? to get the required lack of length, but there shouldn't be too much blousing at the waist. Traditionally, the Is-It-a-Shirt? is worn with thick tights or leggings; the thinner the tights, the more pressing the question of shirtitude. Flat shoes or boots look cute; high heels often change the question from "Is it a shirt?" to something else. Occasionally the Is-It-a-Shirt? is worn as a bathing-suit cover-up, although the farther one is from bodies of water or lounge chairs, the more the Is-It-a-Shirt? should tend toward the dress end of the spectrum.

The Is-It-a-Shirt? is often made from jersey knit (which rides up), lightweight cotton voiles or chambrays (which float up), or denim (which mostly stays in place). In order not to look as if you merely forgot to put on your pants that morning, it helps to accessorize with more jewelry than usual—bangles are customary, but long necklaces (which emphasize the shortness of the dress) work, too.

The Is-It-a-Shirt? is often worn in situations that call for provocation: third dates with men who haven't yet seen fit to make a move, girls' brunches with frenemies, or, if you're fifteen years old, anytime you want to leave the house.

WORN BY: Elaine Stritch, Liza Minnelli, Lindsay Lohan.

49

THE SINGER AND ACTRESS Jennifer Lopez has worn plenty of memorable dresses in her time, but only one deserves the eponymous treatment: the dress she wore to the 2000 Grammys. Designed by Donatella Versace for her fall 1999 collection, the dress was made of sheer silk chiffon with a blue-and-green palm tree print, and it was modeled on the runway by Amber Valletta.

But all that is just trivia compared with the one essential detail of the dress: the wide, deep, breathtaking plunge neckline, ending well below the navel, seemingly held in place only by hope and a jeweled medallion (although industrial quantities of double-stick tape were assumed). The bodice and skirt of the dress were actually attached to a bikini bottom.

The J-Lo dress is quite possibly the Platonic ideal of confidence: confidence in its most pure form. Like Elizabeth Hurley's safety-pin dress of 1994 (also Versace), it was a dress designed to create a commotion, and a commotion was duly created. In the hundreds of photographs of her in that dress, Jennifer Lopez appears completely serene, barely acknowledging the stir she was creating. She didn't say, "Oh, this old thing?" but one could easily imagine her doing so.

If you are going to wear your own version of the J-Lo dress (a style similar in feeling; a knockoff of this particular dress is not recommended), wear it with bravado. Keep everything but the dress simple: you are sounding one note, and no other voices should be heard. Burn your bridges behind you—don't carry a wrap or shawl, don't bring something more conservative "just in case." Brazen through.

RELATED: The Cher.

WORN BY: Jennifer Lopez, Donatella Versace (she wore it herself).

THE JACKIE 50

THE JACKIE DRESS (this refers to the Jackie of White House Jackie Kennedy, not the Jackie of Jackie Kennedy Onassis) is the one you wear when you aren't really supposed to be fashionable but are anyway. The canonical Jackie dress is simultaneously simple and elegant, unexceptionally modest and exceptionally chic.

Unlike the Queen Elizabeth II, which armors the wearer in the apparatus of state, the Jackie dress satisfies the demands of the situation without subsuming itself to them. The Jackie dress treats others' expectations as an interesting artistic constraint to play with, not as shackles to labor under.

While it's possible to adopt the Jackie dress as your own uniform (simple, elegant sleeveless shifts, matching dress-and-coat combos, and long streamlined boatneck gowns will never, ever be out of style), it's better to adopt the Jackie attitude instead. Look at the sartorial expectations and constraints others place on you, and find the loopholes. Your workplace frowns on color? Use shape, and vice versa. Choose a better fabric or silhouette. If the fate of the free world isn't at stake (and it hardly ever is), you may be tempted to just reject the strictures entirely, but resist that urge. Confounding people's expectations while simultaneously checking off all their little boxes can be strangely liberating. (You don't have to be the First Lady to do this—teen girls in school uniforms are experts at obeying the letter rather than the spirit of dress codes.)

ACCESSORIES: Calm confidence and a sly sense of humor, perfect manners, and the escort of a leader of the free world (if you happen to like one).

RELATED: The Queen Elizabeth II.

WORN BY: Jackie Kennedy (of course), Michelle Obama, Carla Bruni, Kate Middleton (at times).

DESIGNERS: Oleg Cassini, Givenchy, Gustave Tassell.

THE MODERN JAPANESE FASHION DRESS is usually dark—black, gray, navy blue—and gives only the slightest indication of the shape of the body under it. (In fact, it may dramatically alter the shape of the body with padding.) Its own shape is often asymmetrical, and the number of armholes may not actually correspond to the number of arms of the wearer. It may be constructed of space-age textiles or tattered cotton.

The most groundbreaking Japanese designers had radically different motivations than Western designers. Rei Kawakubo's first shop for Comme des Garçons in Tokyo didn't have mirrors, to encourage buyers to ignore how the clothes looked and concentrate on how the clothes felt. Issey Miyake's A-POC (for "a piece of cloth") line created clothes from long tubes of jersey, in order to minimize material waste. Yohji Yamamoto blurred gender distinctions by using women as models for his men's line.

Wearers of this kind of Japanese Fashion dress tend to enjoy the cognitive dissonance the clothing creates in both the wearer and the viewer. These clothes require more thought, not just in terms of having to figure out how to put them on but also about what clothing in general is intended to do, once we're past protecting ourselves from the elements and covering (or at least selectively revealing) our nakedness. They're also just as provocative, in their own way, as the lowest-cut evening gown or spikiest Biohazard dress.

ACCESSORIES: Equally thought-provoking, serious, yet comfortable shoes (no pointy stilettos), a hairstyle that defies gravity, and (for the most ragged versions) a tolerance for occasionally being given spare change by people on the street.

RELATED: By geography, the Kimono.

WORN BY: It can be hard to tell who is wearing Japanese designers. As the director John Waters said, "I wear Rei Kawakubo to be fashionable in secret. We know how great her clothes look, but others think we're just poor."

DESIGNERS: Rei Kawakubo (Comme des Garçons), Issey Miyake, Yohji Yamamato.

THE CANONICAL JERSEY SHORE DRESS is tight, bright, and ready for a fight. It doesn't wait for your attention—it steps up to you and pokes a (slightly inebriated) finger into your chest, and says, "'Sup?" The Jersey Shore dress has one goal: to focus as many eyes as possible on the wearer, if only in anticipation of the inevitable wardrobe malfunction.

Although the dress itself is on the small side, everything worn with the Jersey Shore is big: big hair, big sunglasses, big ol' platform shoes, and big attitude. Under it all, of course, is the bare minimum of undergarments and the legal maximum of aggressively tanned skin.

There's a time and place for demure, sweet, frilly, and girlish, but the places that the Jersey Shore dress goes to (and the times it goes to them) are not those times and places. Despite tut-tutting by the fashion police, there's nothing wrong with the aggressive female sexuality that the Jersey Shore embodies (no pun intended). It's also refreshing that the Jersey Shore is often worn by women who are not model-thin. Wearers of the Jersey Shore are confident and unafraid, they know what they want, and they put on that dress to go get it. And if they have to spill a few drinks or push a few paparazzi in the process, so what?

RELATED: The Jersey Shore is a Bandage dress gone bad.

WORN BY: Snooki, J-Woww, etc.

DESIGNERS: Plenty of designers have sent tight, short dresses down the runway, but they don't turn Snooki's head. The *Jersey Shore* star claimed in an interview on the blog *Refinery 29* that she's "not really a designer girl. I still like to shop at Mandees and Forever 21. I don't even look at designers."

THE JUMPER DRESS (known in the UK as a Pinafore dress) is a sleeveless dress intended to be worn over a blouse, shirt, or sweater. A Jumper may have a bodice with a completely closed back, or it may have a bib front, like a pair of overalls.

The Jumper is the endpoint of a long line of women's gowns designed to be worn over a chemise, guimpe, blouse, or other underpinning. It is a favorite style for school and other uniforms, especially for adolescent girls—one women's magazine, in 1914, said that "the new jumper dresses are one of the very best styles for girls of this age. They are decidedly youthful in spite of the fact that they are also worn by women, and what one wants is a style that will still be girlish, for Miss Fourteen-year-old does not wish to suddenly be thrust into the older girls' styles."

It's that youthful quality that makes a Jumper so fun to wear—that, plus the nominative determinism of the very name *jumper*, makes you feel as if you have the boundless and bounding energy of a teenager. (Sorry, Brits, your Pinafore is not quite as much fun.) A Jumper dress—preferably one with capacious pockets—is the perfect Saturday dress. Leave your heavy handbag at home and run out the door with just what you have in your pockets, ready for adventure!

ACCESSORIES: The Jumper is best worn with a simple thin blouse or T-shirt underneath. People don't really wear dickies anymore, but if you're tempted, don't—they only ride up, wrinkle, and twist around. Comfortable flat shoes, especially canvas sneakers or penny loafers, go best with a Jumper, although heeled oxfords can change a Jumper from "teenager" to "librarian" very easily. Wearing high ponytails and sharing milkshakes are completely optional but recommended.

RELATED: The Dirndl.

DESIGNERS: Chloé, Karl Lagerfeld, Marc Jacobs.

THE CLASSIC JUNE CLEAVER DRESS is a cotton button-front shirtwaist with a collar, short sleeves, and a very full skirt.

The June Cleaver is the perfect dress for when you have to both look great and do a lot of tedious, inconvenient, repetitive drudge work—or, in other words, housework and child care. A June Cleaver shirtwaist can do both the grocery shopping and the oven cleaning, with only the addition of the (sometimes matching) apron.

It goes without saying that a pair of jeans (or "dungarees") would often be more comfortable, and that full skirts are not exactly the safest clothing to wear around hot ovens or gas burners, but it's easier to understand the June Cleaver dress if we think of it not as being "at home" but as being "at work." The June Cleaver was, for a long time, the accepted uniform of the occupation put down on the census form as "housewife." And since so many women did (and still do) take justifiable pride in that occupation, it's not surprising that they'd want to look good on the job.

The June Cleaver is also fun to wear—the shirt bodice is neat and comfortable, the full skirt allows for easy movement, the capacious pockets and matching apron are handy, and the number of fabrics you can find one in (everything from staid shirtings to fun ginghams, denims to wild novelty prints) means that almost any taste can be satisfied, even (or especially) that of the man of the house.

ACCESSORIES: Pearls, heels, a vacuum cleaner and/or a plate of freshly baked cookies, and a complete ignorance of the works of Betty Friedan.

WORN BY: Every woman of the 1950s (think Lucille Ball) and vintage-lovers today.

DESIGNER: American sportswear pioneer Claire McCardell is credited with popularizing this style of dress.

THE KIMONO

ALTHOUGH THE SHAPE OF THE KIMONO is elegant and distinctive (and instantly recognizable as Japanese), what the true Kimono devotee cares about is the fabric from which the Kimono is made. Kimono fabric is usually only fourteen inches wide, but it's fourteen inches of some of the most beautiful textiles in the world, and it takes an entire bolt (about twelve and a half yards), cut into seven sections, to make a Kimono. The fabric of some Kimonos (*kimonos* is the English plural, while the Japanese plural is *kimono*; the Japanese word comes from words meaning "thing to wear") is so delicate that Kimonos are traditionally completely disassembled before washing, then put back together again.

Few Japanese wear the Kimono on a daily basis, reserving it for special events—especially since complete Kimono outfits can cost thousands of dollars. Westerners wear the Kimono even more rarely and are almost certain to flub the finer points of Kimono etiquette. Kimono-inspired dresses are widely available, being attractive and comfortable to wear, and the scope their broad flat planes give to showcasing gorgeous fabrics means they show up on the runway season after season.

Anything can be worn in the spirit of the Kimono, though, if you decide to focus less on the traditional garment and more on the ways Kimonos have been used for artistic expression. Gorgeous Japanese textiles such as shibori (a kind of tie-dye), resist-dyed fabrics, and brocades adapt well to Western-style clothes and are extremely satisfying to wear. Kimono style can also highlight connections with the natural world—wearing cherry blossom florals in spring is one obvious example. With a Kimono frame of mind you can make anything you wear into a similar work of art.

WORN BY: Diana Vreeland (in a photograph by Richard Avedon), Elizabeth Taylor (as Flora "Sissy" Goforth in the 1968 film *Boom!*), Lindsay Lohan.

DESIGNERS: Almost every designer has been inspired by the Kimono, including Halston, John Galliano, Yves Saint Laurent, Proenza Schouler, Anna Sui, and others—but not Jason Wu, who said in 2008 that he was more inspired by modern Japan: "Samurais and geishas were a long time ago."

THE LAURA INGALLS WILDER

56

THE LAURA INGALLS WILDER DRESS (the Laura, for short) is any prairie- or frontier-style dress, usually high-necked and long-sleeved with a full, ankle-length skirt, and often made in calico with a floral pattern.

Although the Laura dress is not often worn today (at least, not worn by people who aren't in plural marriages), everyone who grew up on Laura Ingalls Wilder's books still has a fondness for them, and for Wilder's meticulous descriptions of them. In *Little House on the Prairie*, Wilder describes the dress Laura and Ma made for Mary to wear at her school for the blind:

> It was brown cashmere, lined with brown cambric. Small brown buttons buttoned it down the front, and on either side of the buttons and around the bottom Ma had trimmed it with a narrow, shirred strip of brown-and-blue plaid, with red threads and golden threads running through it. A high collar of the plaid was sewed on, and Ma held in her hand a gathered length of white machine-made lace. The lace was to be fitted inside the collar, so that it would fall a little over the top.

The Laura dress is a frontier dress in more ways than one—while her whole family was working to make a living and build a life from their (often inhospitable) homesteading claims, Laura and her mother and sisters were also wresting beauty and fashion from similarly unbroken ground. It didn't matter whether they were living in a dugout or a tarpaper shack; Ma would make sure the girls had clean dresses and neatly braided hair. Their manners would always be closer to "back East" than their homes would ever be again.

ACCESSORIES: An apron, a wide horizon, and (when Ma yells at you) your sunbonnet.

WORN BY: Melissa Gilbert, Chloë Sevigny.

DESIGNERS: Laura Ashley, Band of Outsiders.

THE LEATHER DRESS

57

LEATHER CAN BE USED TO MAKE any shape or style of dress—you can find leather ballgowns, leather shirtwaists, leather dirndls, and even (I suspect) leather muu-muus. But the true Leather dress is the tight, princess-seamed sleeveless or strapless leather minidress.

The Leather dress is associated with the era of 1980s excess (and its cousin, the leather miniskirt, was a staple of music videos). It's everything the 1980s wanted to be: tight, extravagant, show-offy—whether in black or (preferably) dyed some bright color. (Bonus points are given for metallic gold.) The Leather dress wants fast cars, loud music, and as much male attention as possible, and it is the dress of choice for those who don't understand that describing something as "classy" usually means it's not.

The woman in the Leather dress doesn't mind if you think (as the saying goes) that "all her taste is in her mouth." She doesn't really care what you think of her, but if you're thinking of her at all, she would like those thoughts to be envious ones.

ACCESSORIES: High heels, supermodel hair, slightly too much gold jewelry, and aplomb.

WORN BY: Stephanie Seymour (and other supermodel types), Emma Stone, Brooklyn Decker, Beyoncé (the Leather dress is making a comeback, especially among those too young to remember its hair-metal days), Blake Lively.

DESIGNERS: Versace (of course), Céline (slightly more tasteful).

THE LET'S GO ICE DANCING!

THERE IS A CERTAIN KIND of dress that subscribes to the belief that more is more—more sequins, more spangles, more lace, more ruffles, more stretch, more flip to the skirt. Usually these dresses are seen in sports where feminine decorativeness is part of the contest, especially competitive ballroom dancing, ice skating, and ice dancing. "Go for the gold" refers not just to the medal but to the use of lamé.

The Let's Go Ice Dancing! dress, then, is what happens when the styles suitable for those sports escape the floor and the rink, lengthen their skirts, and head out into the world. These dresses tend to show up at other events where convention plays a significant role, particularly weddings and proms. Especially proms. Did I say proms?

It makes sense, of course, that Let's Go Ice Dancing! dresses would show up at proms. Proms are often the occasion of the first "fancy" dress, and years spent marveling at besequined heroines can build up until they overflow into a dress that suffers from a serious overload of "fancy."

It's entirely possible to have a tasteful Let's Go Ice Dancing! dress—the main distinctive feature borrowed from competition versions is the use of sheer illusion netting, especially to give a strapless or near-strapless effect. When done in black, with a fuller pencil skirt, it can look surprisingly elegant.

ACCESSORIES: Extremely vibrant eye shadow and rhinestone or glitter makeup, slicked-back hair, industrial-strength tights, and, occasionally, a soundtrack of Ravel's "Boléro."

RELATED: The Disney, the Lolita.

DESIGNERS: Stella McCartney used polka-dot illusion netting to dramatic effect in a 2011 dress worn by Kate Winslet, Susan Sarandon, Liv Tyler, and even Jane Fonda.

IN THE WEST, the name Lolita has definite sexual overtones, thanks to the novel by Vladimir Nabokov, but in Japan, Lolita style (often abbreviated as *loli*) focuses more on girlishness and not at all on skeevy older men.

Lolita clothes in general are heavily influenced by Victorian and Rococo style—dresses with full skirts (often given a cupcake shape with crinolines), pinafores, lots of lace, and bonnets or hats. The idea is to look as much like a fancy doll as humanly possible. Lolita style variants include Sweet Lolitas—more cutesy, with more bows, more ruffles, more polka dots, and more references to Hello Kitty; Country Lolitas, who like jumpers, gingham, fruit patterns, and straw baskets and hats; and Guro Lolitas, who try for a "broken doll" look with fake blood, slings, and bandages (*guro* means "gore"). Goth Lolitas (often written *gothloli*) favor darker colors and more gothy accessories: bats, skulls, coffins, and so on. The Elegant Gothic Lolitas (a term coined by Japanese musician Mana) prefer more monochromatic color combinations and longer silhouettes.

The style may seem over-the-top and strange, but it's a near certainty that Lolitas are having more fun with their clothes than you are. The emphasis on self-expression (many *lolis* design and sew their own outfits), the community support for especially creative and interesting combinations, and the sheer fun of full skirts, giant bows, and hats make for a more joyous relationship with clothes. And because the foundation of the style is aggressively childlike and nonsexual, *lolis* can't be accused of simply seeking male attention. The style gives the best of both worlds—the sense of fun and play associated with childlike clothes, and the opportunity for autonomy and self-creation available to adults.

ACCESSORIES: Cell phones, stickers, sausage-curled or bobbed hair, tourists taking your photo.

RELATED: The Let's Go Ice Dancing!, the Dorothy, the Baby Doll.

DESIGNERS: Often the wearers themselves, although Sarah Ruth (for Sweet Lolitas) and Naoto Hirooka (of the h.NAOTO brand) are well known.

60

THE DRESS WORN BY MADAME X—the mysterious, alluring woman of John Singer Sargent's 1884 *Portrait de Mme ****—is a column of lush black velvet, contrasting strongly with the expanse of pale shoulder and décolletage that it leaves bare.

Madame X (as Sargent later titled the picture) was not unknown. She was Madame Gautreau (née Virginie Amélie Avegno, known as Amélie), an American expatriate from New Orleans who, at nineteen, married the wealthy (and unusually short) forty-year-old bat-guano magnate Pierre-Louis Gautreau. She was famous in Paris for her beauty—newspapers reported on her gowns, including a salmon-colored velvet—and supposedly King Ludwig II of Bavaria made a special trip to the Paris Opéra just to see Amélie walk up the staircase there.

Sargent wanted his portrait of Madame Gautreau to win him public acclaim and lucrative commissions for other portraits; Amélie wanted—we think—to be immortalized as a great beauty and to be the object of other women's envy. Neither got exactly what they wanted. The critics hated the portrait—they thought Sargent's treatment of Amélie's artificially whitened, almost lavender skin "nauseating" and the picture "vulgar." The original portrait showed one strap slipping from her shoulder (Sargent later retouched it), and that detail led to Amélie herself being made the subject of satirical and insulting cartoons, showing her with a bare bosom, and for some time afterward in Paris dresses with slipping straps were said to have necklines "à la Gautreau."

Of course, modern viewers of Sargent's painting usually know nothing of this—they see the transcendently, almost eerily beautiful woman in a long dark velvet evening gown. The essential beauty of the dress has outlived its creator, its wearer, its immortalizer, and all of its (and their) critics, which is what we hope true things of beauty will always do: persist, whatever the odds.

The Madame X dress is worn with an eye to the long game rather than short-term results.

WORN BY: Angelina Jolie is the modern incarnation of Madame X.

DESIGNER: The original dress was designed by Félix, a former hairdresser and one of the foremost couturiers of his time. His full name was Félix Poussineau.

THE MAE WEST/JOAN HOLLOWAY

THE MAE WEST/JOAN HOLLOWAY dress is any dress that's designed to show off an hourglass figure, especially an extreme hourglass. What's an extreme hourglass? *Hollywood* magazine in 1937 compared Mae West's figure to that of the Venus de Milo, though Mae was an inch bigger at the bust, at 35 inches, and an inch smaller in the waist, at 27½, than that classical ideal. Christina Hendricks, the actress who plays Joan Holloway on *Mad Men*, is supposedly 39-30-39 (according to slavering fans on the Internet).

The woman who wears the Mae West/Joan Holloway dress has usually come to terms with having an unfashionable body type (I said unfashionable, not unattractive; studies show that men, at least, are most attracted to a waist-hip ratio of about 0.7). Designers don't usually design for the true hourglass, and high-fashion models don't fall into that category, either. There's an art to dressing an hourglass figure, and women who want to show theirs off know how frustrating practicing that art can be. Proper fit is essential, lest that eye-popping waist-hip ratio be swallowed up by excess fabric. So Mae/Joan types learn to be choosy and buy only well-made clothes that lend themselves to easy alterations.

If you're going to catch the eye anyway (and you will if you fill out a Mae West/Joan Holloway dress), you should make the most of it. Wear bright colors, especially red. Wear high heels, if you like them. The Mae West/Joan Holloway dress is the ultimate in "if you've got it, flaunt it."

ACCESSORIES: Long, dangling charms and chains draw the eye up and down your curves.

RELATED: The Madame X, the Siren.

WORN BY: Jean Harlow, Elizabeth Taylor, Kim Kardashian, Jessica Rabbit, Mae West, Christina Hendricks.

THERE ARE LOTS OF DRESSES associated with Marilyn Monroe—the "Happy Birthday, Mr. President" gold sheath and the pink "Diamonds Are a Girl's Best Friend" strapless number both spring to mind—but the canonical Marilyn dress is the one she wore in the 1955 Billy Wilder movie *The Seven Year Itch*.

The iconic shot is of Marilyn, in a white halter dress, standing over a subway grate as the updraft from the train whooshing by blows up her pleated skirt. The dress was designed by William Travilla ("Billy" to Marilyn, but known professionally just as "Travilla"), who also designed costumes for Marlene Dietrich, Loretta Young, Jane Russell, and Judy Garland. The actress Debbie Reynolds bought the original dress from the studio, and it sold at auction for $4.6 million in 2011.

The swingy skirt and flattering halter make anyone feel like Marilyn Monroe, which is probably why reproductions, in both the original white and many other prints and colors, are widely available. The Marilyn-style halter is enormous fun to wear, with or without a passing draft to give onlookers a thrill.

ACCESSORIES: White strappy sandals, white brief-style underwear (which you keep in your freezer), a sense of playfulness.

RELATED: The Siren, the Baby Doll.

THE MARY QUANT

MARY QUANT IS ONE OF TWO DESIGNERS credited with inventing the mini-skirt (the other was André Courrèges), although she refused to claim it, saying, "It wasn't me or Courrèges who invented the miniskirt anyway—it was the girls in the street who did it." But the girls in the street wanted to look like Mary Quant, with her Vidal Sassoon haircut, the tights she sold in unusual colors such as "ginger" and "prune" (she had to have them made by a theatrical costumer for her London boutique, Bazaar), and especially her easy, youthful dresses. Some dresses were reminiscent of children's clothes, such as the gray wool jumper-and-blouse combination that won the first annual Dress of the Year vote from the Fashion Museum in Bath in 1963, but the classic Quant dress is the easy, shiftlike minidress (named after her favorite car, the Mini).

To wear a Mary Quant dress is to feel yourself, if only for a moment, in the swinging London where it was born. You shrug off the last of the postwar malaise and ride off on a scooter, late for a rock show or some kind of "happening." In a Mary Quant you will be young and hip forever, no matter what your grumbling elders say.

ACCESSORIES: You should wear your Mary Quant dress with bright plastic jewelry, colored tights, square-heeled shoes, and just a little too short for your mother's taste.

RELATED: The Baby Doll, the Face.

WORN BY: Mia Farrow (in *Rosemary's Baby*), Audrey Hepburn (in *Two for the Road*), the salesgirls at Sir Terence Conran's Habitat shop in London.

DESIGNERS: Mary Quant, André Courrèges.

THE MATERNITY

MATERNITY "FASHION" IS A RECENT INVENTION—before World War II, maternity clothing mostly involved moving fastenings around and (as uncomfortable as it sounds) switching to less-restrictive corsets. Maternity wear, if it was mentioned at all, was often euphemized with phrases such as "for the recently married lady," and it was never shown on an obviously pregnant figure. But with the postwar baby boom, merchandisers sensed an opportunity and were less reticent about advertising maternity wear, so catalogs and stores began to carry skirts with stretchy panels and smocklike dresses and overblouses.

The stereotypical maternity dress of the latter half of the twentieth century looks as if it were made for a freakishly tall kindergartener who has accidentally swallowed a bowling ball. Childlike details such as bows, Peter Pan collars, and polka dots abounded, and dresses were often made in soft pinks and blues or ginghams. It seemed as if in order to have a baby, you had to regress to dressing like one yourself.

Luckily, modern maternity dresses have largely abandoned that look, becoming much more body-conscious and showing off the "baby bump" rather than hiding it.

ACCESSORIES: The happiness due to an expectant mother, and the dawning realization that you will now be the target of unsolicited parenting advice for the rest of your life.

RELATED: The Baby Doll.

DESIGNERS: Liz Lange is credited with kick-starting the designer maternity market, and publicized her designs by offering them to Cindy Crawford, Gwyneth Paltrow, and other expectant stars. Now designers of maternity wear include the celebrity moms themselves, such as Heidi Klum, Jessica Simpson, and Nicole Richie.

WE MEET MISS HAVISHAM in Dickens's *Great Expectations* through the eyes of the boy Pip:

> She was dressed in rich materials,—satins, and lace, and silks,—all of white. Her shoes were white. And she had a long white veil dependent from her hair, and she had bridal flowers in her hair, but her hair was white. Some bright jewels sparkled on her neck and on her hands, and some other jewels lay sparkling on the table. Dresses, less splendid than the dress she wore, and half-packed trunks, were scattered about. She had not quite finished dressing, for she had but one shoe on,—the other was on the table near her hand,—her veil was but half arranged, her watch and chain were not put on, and some lace for her bosom lay with those trinkets, and with her handkerchief, and gloves, and some flowers, and a Prayer-Book all confusedly heaped about the looking-glass.

The Miss Havisham dress is any garment worn well past its proper moment, out of time and out of place, clung to as a remnant of some past happiness never to be regained. Whether it's as dramatic as keeping the dress you were wearing when you learned you were jilted or as banal as holding on to the polyester satin prom dress from the year you were homecoming queen, the Miss Havisham dress inspires both ridicule and pity, depending on how far removed in time is the event that fixed the wearer like a fly in sartorial amber.

ACCESSORIES: An air of being hard done by or of outright delusion, with increasing desperation and difficulty as time passes, ancient inedible cake.

DESIGNERS: Modern designers such as Prabal Gurung and Georgina Chapman (of Marchesa) have cited Miss Havisham as a reference or an inspiration.

THE MODERN BRIDE

THE MODERN BRIDE has a visceral reaction to Cinderella-style or Cupcake Bride–type dresses, and that reaction is not jumping up and down, clapping, in happy tears. It is more akin to a bad case of hives. She is thrilled to be getting married and excited about her wedding, but she doesn't see why a wedding dress has to be so very far removed from everyday clothing. If put to the test, the Modern Bride would rather look like Princess Leia than Princess Diana.

The Modern Bride dress says that the wearer prefers her own personality and taste to the conventions of the wedding-industrial complex and is determined enough to stick to them. Sometimes the Modern Bride is on her second (or third) wedding and has already done the giant frou-frou dress, sometimes the Modern Bride prefers striking to sentimental, and sometimes the Modern Bride just doesn't look that good in white.

All sorts of dresses can qualify as "Modern Bride"—actual modernity, in the form of quirky asymmetrical columns; colorful, festive ethnic costumes (especially those of an ethnicity you don't actually share); retro dressmaker suits and vintage evening gowns; or any dress that has special meaning to the couple. Why not get married in the dress you wore on your first date, if that's what you want?

The Modern Bride dress is worn with the emphasis on the "something new," although borrowed and blue do often make appearances.

ACCESSORIES: The Modern Bride is unlikely to wear garters, crinolines, embellished flat tennis shoes, or cathedral-length veils, but hardly anyone can resist a tiara.

WORN BY (AND DESIGNED BY): Women musicans (and women marrying musicians) seem to have greater leeway in choosing unconventional attire: Dita von Teese wore a purple Vivienne Westwood dress for her 2005 wedding to Marilyn Manson, Gwen Stefani wore a pink and white dress by John Galliano at her 2002 wedding to Gavin Rossdale, Kelis wore a dress in shades of green designed by Matthew Williamson at her 2005 wedding to Nas, and Pamela Anderson wore a white string bikini (designer unknown) when marrying Kid Rock in 2006.

THE MONDRIAN DRESS was designed by Yves Saint Laurent as part of his "Mondrian Look" collection of 1965, inspired (of course) by the Dutch painter Piet Mondrian. By any measure, it was a resounding success: it made the cover of *Vogue*, and it was copied so much (as was Saint Laurent's other landmark design, the smoking, or women's tuxedo) that it led the designer to open up his own ready-to-wear line, Saint Laurent Rive Gauche, the following year. (The thinking was that if anyone was going to be making money from noncouture versions, it might as well be the original designer.)

The dress was a technological feat as well as an artistic one, since Saint Laurent had to hide all the dress shaping inside the seams of the grid design—he didn't want the shaping to be visible, as it would have undercut the ideal of flatness he was aiming to achieve by referencing Mondrian. (Saint Laurent, always trying to "rethink and refine," revisited the Mondrian idea in a jacket in his 1979 collection.) The Mondrian dress is still popular today, and knockoffs and how-tos for making your own are easy to find.

ACCESSORIES: Dark or flesh-tone tights, square-heeled shoes or go-go boots, a short, swingy Sassoon-style haircut, and the confidence that comes from knowing that you're a work of art.

RELATED: The Face, the Mary Quant.

WORN BY: Jean Shrimpton and so many others that in 1970, *New York* magazine pronounced it "so boringly popular."

THE MOURET   **68**

IN HIS SPRING 2006 COLLECTION, French designer Roland Mouret showed what he called the Galaxy dress. With a square neckline, a defined waist, and a softly puffed cap sleeve, in saturated jewel tones, glen plaids, and the inevitable chic black, it's been called the "dress of the decade."

The Mouret dress was so overwhelmingly popular because it managed to combine a ladylike demeanor with a vamp silhouette. The dress's external shell was a wool-Lycra or rayon-Lycra blend, but the lining was a tough, stretchy material called Powerflex, which turned it into something that was essentially a girdle. The dress helped to create the very curves that it highlighted, and everyone wanted one. Those who couldn't afford the original (which was in limited supply and cost thousands of dollars) ran to the mass-market knockoffs, available at every department store. There was even a knockoff dress pattern for home sewers. A 2011 reissue sparked intense demand and long waiting lists.

Mouret has said that the inspiration for this dress came from feedback from women who were tired of dresses that couldn't be worn with a bra. He then realized that dresses were "about women, it's not about five minutes on a catwalk." Like Chanel, Mouret looked at what women's lives were actually like, and designed for their everyday needs. The Mouret fills a gap that many women have in their wardrobe: a serious dress that is also seriously sexy, without showing acres of cleavage or thigh, and that doesn't require buying special underwear or going without.

ACCESSORIES: A narrow leather belt, expensive high-heeled shoes (Louboutins by preference), and the kind of smugness that can only be conveyed by an expensive designer dress that is also indisputably flattering.

RELATED: The Airship Hostess, the Chanel Jersey dress.

WORN BY: Just about everyone who could get their hands on one, including Rachel Weisz, Cameron Diaz, Sienna Miller, Demi Moore, Scarlett Johansson, Miranda Kerr, Dita von Teese, and Victoria Beckham, who hired the pattern cutter for her own line based on a recommendation from Mouret.

THE NOVEMBER RAIN DRESS was born in the video for the Guns N' Roses song of the same name. As worn by model Stephanie Seymour (Seymour and singer Axl Rose met on the set of the video and began dating), the dress has a bodice that is fairly conventional—a sweetheart neckline with off-the-shoulder short puffed sleeves. It's the skirt that makes the dress perfect for a rock-and-roll video, echoing the classic mullet: short in the front, long in the back. Very short in the front—micromini, a good ten inches above the knee. (In the video, Seymour's garter is clearly visible.) The dress was designed by Carmela Sutera and reportedly cost $8,000. The dress and the video were both hugely popular—MTV placed the video at number one in their list of the top one hundred videos of 1992, and replicas of the dress are still for sale today.

The wearer of the November Rain dress is a bit of a wild child—wild in conventional, stereotypical ways, but still wild. She may be getting married and succumbing to the pull of tradition, but she's doing it her way, and she's going to rock out.

ACCESSORIES: Rocker groom, wailing guitars, supermodel legs.

WORN BY: Stephanie Seymour, brides who re-create the dress for their special day (no, really, it's a thing—Google it).

DESIGNER: Carmela Sutera.

THE PEGGY OLSON (after the character on AMC's *Mad Men*) is a classic midcentury dress. Its most distinguishing characteristics are a long tight line from neck to hip, a prim and missish collar, short sleeves, a fullish skirt, and some kind of juvenile ornamentation, especially a bow.

The Peggy Olson is worn in a state of semiarrested development: it emphasizes womanly curves but satisfies a taste that hasn't quite left the schoolroom. Peggy Olson gets straight A's, and she always raises her hand when the teacher asks a question. She won't play along with a prank, but she won't tell, either. Peggy Olson blushes and gets inconvenient fits of the giggles, then burns with humiliation at acting like a child . . . and then gets up the next day and does it again.

The Peggy Olson dress serves as training wheels: a way to take a maturing body out for a little spin without getting into too much trouble. It stops short of outlining the rear, after all, and doesn't reveal any actual cleavage. The Peggy Olson is the fruity drink of dresses: the sweetness covers up the kick. The Peggy Olson usually doesn't last much past a woman's mid-twenties or her first serious romantic relationship, whichever comes first.

ACCESSORIES: A ponytail, sensible low-heeled shoes, a clean handkerchief, an earnest expression, a dawning realization that hard work and honesty aren't all that matters.

RELATED: The June Cleaver.

WORN BY: Countless unsung office workers of the 1950s and 1960s.

DESIGNERS: Anne Fogarty, Claire McCardell (for Townley, in particular).

THE POLO DRESS 71

THE POLO DRESS, like the Shirtdress and the T-Shirt dress, is another garment that started in the men's clothing column before lengthening itself into dress status. The Polo dress takes its name from the polo shirt, which is generally credited to French tennis player René Lacoste. Lacoste created a knit shirt with a soft collar and button placket for tennis players in the early 1930s, and it was available only in white until 1951. (The polo players adopted it once they saw how comfortable it was.) The term "polo collar" has several meanings: it includes what is called a "turtleneck" in the United States and also what we now know as the "button-down collar." (Polo players liked variety in their necklines, it seems.)

The Polo dress—with or without a logo—has become a classic piece of American sportswear, and as such, it is perfect for classic American outings, which very rarely include watching or playing polo. Wear your Polo dress to picnics, cookouts, and barbecues; for running errands and shopping; in most business-casual workplaces—basically, everywhere. The Polo dress says, "I like being neatly put together and comfortable, but a T-Shirt dress is a little too sloppy for me."

ACCESSORIES: It's impossible to get away from the aura of WASPy preppiness that surrounds the Polo dress, so you might as well not even try—go ahead and wear it with a ribbon headband, a Bermuda bag, Tretorn sneakers or Jack Rogers sandals, a canvas or braided leather belt, and a Nantucket rope bracelet. But if you can avoid it by any means, please don't pop the collar.

RELATED: The Cowgirl, the Is-It-a-Shirt?, the Shirtdress, the T-Shirt dress.

WORN BY: Mean girls in 1980s teen movies, moms who live in places whose names begin with "Palm."

DESIGNERS: Ralph Lauren, Lacoste.

THE PRETTY WOMAN

THE 1990 PROBLEMATIC SEMI-ROMANCE movie *Pretty Woman* is full of "clothes moments"—there's a red opera dress, there's a hooker outfit, there's an Audrey-worthy black cocktail dress. There's also a much-quoted shopping moment, where Julia Roberts, who plays prostitute Vivian Ward, tells a snotty Rodeo Drive shopgirl, "Do you remember me, the person you refused to wait on yesterday [when she was wearing thigh-high black vinyl boots]? Big mistake. Huge."

But the truly pivotal dress in the movie is the brown-and-white polka-dot dress worn at the polo match. Costume designer Marilyn Vance designed and made all the dresses for the movie herself, and told *Elle* magazine she had found exactly enough fabric for the dress in the basement of a fabric store in Beverly Hills. By making the dress just a bit shorter than originally intended (and having Julia Roberts wear heels instead of flats) she had enough left over for the matching hat.

The dress itself was much in demand—two years after the film came out, versions were available at Laura Ashley, JC Penney, and Charlotte Russe, at prices ranging from $40 to almost $140.

The Pretty Woman dress is any dress that serves both to hide one's origins and to bring out some essential truth of character. Vivian is not a wealthy polo fan, but she is a kindhearted person—and if gentility is good manners, and good manners are (as Emily Post puts it) "a sensitive awareness of the feelings of others," Vivian is just as genteel as those around her, and possibly more so.

It's difficult to set out to wear a Pretty Woman dress—they kind of sneak up on us when we're not looking. We may try to wear something to fit in, and only later find that it has revealed something that sets us apart.

ACCESSORIES: A matching hat, a heart of gold.

RELATED: The Pretty Woman dress is a direct descendant of the dress worn to Ascot by Eliza Doolittle in *My Fair Lady*.

THE QUEEN ELIZABETH I   *73*

THE SIGNAL CHARACTERISTIC of the Queen Elizabeth I dress is the ruff. The ruff sets off the face like a frame or a halo, and is (as the very best fashions sometimes are) completely impractical. Enormous effort was needed to create and maintain Elizabethan ruffs—they needed starch (at the time very few people even knew how to do the "clear starching" ruffs required, and those were mostly Dutch or Flemish immigrants). Those who couldn't afford starch propped up their ruffs with wire frames. Ruffs needed special goffering irons to press them, and special frames to make them on. Ruffs were made of cambric or lawn, both of which were very expensive. Some were jeweled or embroidered. Later sources have claimed (without proof) that some ladies needed spoons two feet long to maneuver past their ruffs, and it's not pleasant to think of how desperately unsanitary an often-worn, seldom-washed ruff must have been. All this made them easy to criticize—one carper called them "cartwheels in the Devil's chariot of pride," and they were also known as "millstones" for their size and shape.

But what better dress for a queen than one that displayed in a single dramatic accessory the extent of her wealth and her power? In order not to be outruffed by the ladies of the court, Queen Elizabeth regulated the width of ruffs, and supposedly there were ruff monitors at the city gates who had license to measure the ruffs of people entering, and to cut off the excess of those found to be exceeding the limits. The limits were generous—ruffs were often nearly fifteen inches across and two or three rows deep.

If you choose to wear a ruff, it's best to keep the rest of your outfit simple (you won't be able to see much of it over your ruff, anyhow). The ruff is worn with the conviction of absolute power, which, over time, is much more chafing than any piece of starched linen.

DESIGNERS: Moschino, Gianfranco Ferré, and Karl Lagerfeld (for Chanel) are some of the Elizabeth-inspired designers who have shown ruffs on the runway.

THE QUEEN ELIZABETH II

74

QUEEN ELIZABETH II has been declared by no less an authority than designer Miuccia Prada as "one of the most elegant women in the world," which is no small feat when you think of all the external constraints she has on her wardrobe. Although the queen could patronize any designer in the world, she must restrict herself to designers from the British Isles. Her shoes must always have low, square heels—she does a lot of standing. She has to wear color—she once remarked, "I can't wear beige because people won't know who I am." (Clear pastels show off her jewels; strong bright colors make her visible even in large crowds.) Her dresses often have to incorporate symbolic gestures—not just her coronation dress, which included an embroidered shamrock for Northern Ireland, a leek for Wales, and a protea for South Africa, among other national-flower motifs, but her clothes for other occasions as well. A 1957 dress worn to a state dinner in Ottawa included velvet maple leaves, and an evening gown worn in Pakistan featured that country's national colors, ivory and emerald green. (The queen doesn't get to avoid colors she doesn't look good in; matters of state take precedence).

The queen's outfits are engineered like the armor they are: her hats all come with matching hatpins, so they never blow off, and her skirts are weighted with curtain weights or lengths of chain, so a gust of wind never reveals anything. Her dresses are made of fabrics that resist creasing (and once, after an inadvertent soaking, she refused to sit down so that her dress would not wrinkle as it dried). The bright colors, strong fabrics, and weighted hems she wears are as much a part of the queen's protective detail as the bulletproof glass of the Popemobile or the Secret Service men who shadow the president of the United States.

A Queen Elizabeth II dress is anything you wear primarily to fulfill other people's expectations of you—duty dresses, if you will. Despite the wearer's high station, they're worn with the kind of humility that comes with putting your responsibilities before your own desires. (Other examples of obligation garments include mother-of-the-groom dresses, jewelry made for you by your children, and sweaters knitted for you by well-meaning but unstylish relatives).

ACCESSORIES: A handbag . . . but what's in it?

RELATED: The Jackie, the Queen Elizabeth I.

DESIGNERS: Norman Hartnell, Hardy Amies, Angela Kelly.

75

THE ROSIE OF THE ROSIE'S DAY OFF DRESS is Rosie the Riveter. Although she spent her working shifts in overalls, her hair pinned back in a bandanna, on her days off she wanted to wear a dress.

What kind of dress Rosie could wear was bounded by the hard edges of what was available, due to the government's wartime restrictions on fabric availability and manufacturing. Limits on how many yards of fabric could be used for a single dress meant that skirts were slim (no more than 72 inches in circumference at the hem) and fairly short, just past the knee. They had a hem depth of no more than two inches, as compared with the prewar manufacturing standard of three. Sleeves were short, and even pockets and belts were restricted, with belts not allowed to exceed two inches in width. American manufacturers made even slimmer and shorter dresses than the regulations required, saving another fifteen million yards of fabric for the war effort . . . although the dresses were different enough from earlier fashions that people felt some pressure to wear the new "patriotic" styles, somewhat defeating the purpose of those fabric-saving strategies.

The stereotypical Rosie dress is a shirtwaist dress with broad shoulders and a knee-length (or even shorter) skirt, worn with cork-soled fabric shoes (since leather and rubber were both scarce), an elaborate hairstyle (such as pin curls or victory rolls), and a brave "I can do it" attitude. That attitude is so ingrained in this style of dress that even modern wearers have been known to stand a little straighter and try a little harder in a design of 1940s vintage.

WORN BY: Paloma Picasso famously wore flea-market 1940s finds in the late 1960s.

DESIGNERS: Marc Jacobs, Anna Sui, Jean Paul Gaultier. The 1940s revival was credited to Yves Saint Laurent (who in 1971 called an entire collection "Hommage aux Années 40"—Homage to the Forties).

THE SACK DRESS was a late-1950s innovation that came in reaction to the "New Look" of tight waists and full skirts. The Sack, or chemise, had no waistline at all and was roundly despised by men, who saw in the hiding of the female form a Communist plot. Adlai Stevenson said that it came from Moscow, and Bob Hope joked that Russian women, dowdy by American standards, had "been wearing sack dresses for years." Popular culture (including a song, "In the Sack" by Jerry Herman) made much of the fact that, inside the Sack dress, a woman's essential figure was indiscernible. (Anita Loos wrote that no man was going to "puzzle his brain" over the shape of a girl in a bikini.) Designed by Balenciaga and Givenchy (who were likely inspired by Paul Poiret) and championed by Carmel Snow, the editor of *Harper's Bazaar*, the dress proved very popular and was widely copied at every price point.

The message of the Sack dress is one of fashion over allure: it's a dress notable for repelling male attention, to which the wearer says, "So what?" Wearers of the Sack dress would rather be chic than sexy, rather be free than fancied.

ACCESSORIES: Kitten heels, a kicky hat, large earrings, gloves, and a healthy disregard for men's opinions.

RELATED: The Caftan.

WORN BY: Audrey Hepburn (especially in the Givenchy versions), the Duchess of Windsor, Doris Day.

THE SAFARI DRESS was launched into the realm of fashion perennials with Yves Saint Laurent's 1968 Saharienne collection, which included a safari look. His take was not a dress but a tunic/jacket, just long enough so the more daring could wear it as a dress . . . and there were plenty of the more daring around to do exactly that. The Safari dress, with its laces, epaulettes, straps, belts, and pockets, promised exotic adventure (with the barest whiff of colonialism).

The Safari dress hints that you just might be dangerous, and that even the kings of the jungle aren't safe from you. Maybe you haven't traveled to Africa or hunted anything that couldn't be subdued with a high-limit credit card, but a Safari dress will make you look as if you had.

The Safari cycles in and out of fashion at cicadalike intervals, with remarkably little variation. A simple khaki Shirtdress with epaulettes and patch pockets should see you through several Safari-dress campaigns.

ACCESSORIES: Knee-high (or thigh-high) boots, aviator sunglasses, a headscarf, and (if you are feeling matchy-matchy) YSL's Saharienne perfume. Unless you are actually out shooting big game (in which case a couture dress is probably out of place), do not take a gun.

WORN BY: Lauren Hutton, most of the 1970s jet set.

DESIGNERS: Yves Saint Laurent, Banana Republic (before it was taken over by the Gap), Ralph Lauren.

SOURCES DIFFER AS TO HOW MANY ways it's possible to drape a Sari, but it's generally agreed that all of them are beautiful. The word *sari* comes from a Sanskrit word meaning "strip of cloth," and a long piece of cloth, up to nine yards long, is the main component of the Sari (and no, that's not where the phrase "the whole nine yards" comes from).

Everyday modern Saris are usually worn in the Nivi style, over a tight-fitting bodice (or *choli*) and a petticoat skirt tied at the waist with a drawstring. The *pallu* (or endpiece) of the Sari is arranged in pleats and hangs over the back of the left shoulder. The *pallu* is a very versatile part of the garment, useful for covering one's head, as a convenient handhold for a toddler, or as an easy way to grab a hot pan, and it can be tucked in at the waist to prepare for any strenuous activity or argument.

The glory of the Sari, however, is not just in the beautiful folds but in the often-spectacular fabrics used to make those folds. In glowing colors, embroidered or embellished with jewels or mirrors, bordered in patterns created with gold thread, in silk or cotton, figured or plain . . . it's impossible to see a Sari and not want to have one of your own.

Although the Sari hasn't made as much headway into daily Western dress as the Cheongsam (or, to a lesser extent, the Kimono), the popularity of Bollywood movies has made them more familiar, if not less exotic. It's still difficult for Westerners to wear a Sari without looking costumey, but not difficult at all to appreciate their beauty. If you do have a chance to wear a Sari, wear it with mindfulness—it would be a shame to be draped in all that gorgeous fabric and not enjoy every single minute of it.

WORN BY: Liz Hurley, Padma Lakshmi, Angelina Jolie, Helen Mirren, Madonna, Ashley Judd.

DESIGNERS: Matthew Williamson, Thakoon Panichgul, Jean Paul Gaultier.

The moss-green curtains felt prickly and soft beneath her cheek and she rubbed her face against them gratefully, like a cat. And then suddenly she looked at them.

—Margaret Mitchell, *Gone with the Wind*

SCARLETT O'HARA NEEDS MONEY for the taxes on Tara, and she doesn't have a dress fit to wear . . . until she looks up and sees those green velvet curtains. A bit of work turns them into something that Rhett Butler, her intended target, says makes Scarlett "look like the Rue de la Paix." Rhett doesn't succumb, but the green dress finds Scarlett a husband anyway, and so what if he was engaged to her sister? Scarlett will think about that later.

A replica of the dress used in the movie, commissioned by the Harry Ransom Humanities Research Center at the University of Texas at Austin (which holds the archives of director David O. Selznick), took more than two hundred hours to make and used sixteen yards of Italian cotton velveteen. The "curtain dress" has turned into a trope of television and film, most famously from *The Carol Burnett Show*, where Bob Mackie made a curtain dress for Carol that included the curtain rods. (The line Carol Burnett delivered in it: "I saw it in the window and I just couldn't resist it.")

The Scarlett O'Hara dress doesn't have to be made from velvet curtains; it can be any dress you scrounge together in a time of great need. The defining characteristic of the Scarlett O'Hara is not the fabric of the dress but the determination of the wearer.

ACCESSORIES: Whatever you can put together that makes a good show, including a callous disregard for others' feelings, but most of all what Scarlett would call "gumption."

THE SHIRTDRESS

80

THE SHIRTDRESS, in its most classic form, looks much like a man's dress shirt, just longer. It has a stand collar, buttons down the front, and often a shirttail hem, barrel cuffs, and occasionally even a breast pocket. A close relative of the Shirtdress is the shirtwaist dress (see the June Cleaver), which is a shirtlike bodice attached to a fuller skirt.

The Shirtdress is always chic, streamlined, and elegant. It can be dressed down by pairing it with sneakers and rolling up the sleeves, or dressed up with more impressive jewelry and a blazer. Shirtdresses are (no surprise) most often made with shirting cottons, but you can find ones in every fabric (even satin, although satin Shirtdresses tend to look more like pajamas than streetwear) and in almost every length, from mini to nearly ankle length.

The key to the Shirtdress is keeping the slight androgyny of such a male item of clothing in balance with the female form. A Shirtdress should never be baggy enough to suggest that you have actually lifted a guy's shirt from his closet, nor should it be so tight that it gapes and pulls—it should always fit well at the bust and hip.

ACCESSORIES: The Shirtdress is worn with simple shoes (loafers, ballet flats, or plain pumps), and classic bags and jewelry. Your accessories should suggest classic menswear, not the bleeding edge of fashion, and casual hairstyles are best. The Shirtdress can be worn belted or unbelted, and it is occasionally cinched with a man's tie as a belt, although very few women can get away with wearing a Shirtdress with a man's tie as a tie without looking like a drag-king clown who's lost his pants.

RELATED: The June Cleaver, the Cowgirl, the Is-It-a-Shirt?, the Polo dress, the T-Shirt dress.

DESIGNERS: Modern interpreters of the Shirtdress include Narciso Rodriguez, Peter Som, Isaac Mizrahi, and Thakoon Panichgul, among others.

THE SIREN

THE SIREN DRESS evokes a combination of the Sirens of Greek mythology, who sang men to their deaths, and the siren on top of the ambulance, red and flashing. The Siren dress can be any length, silhouette, or fabric, as long as it's red . . . and as long as it's intended to lure men to their doom.

It may sound like hokum, but it's science. A 2011 study found that men rated women wearing red as being more interested in sex—and the women weren't wearing slinky dresses, they were wearing red T-shirts. Scientists theorize that connecting the color red with sexual receptiveness is a holdover from early primate biology, where females in estrus have red faces (and other body parts) due to open blood vessels caused by high estrogen levels. Science also tells us that if you really want to arouse a man, skip the perfume and try to smell like pumpkin pie instead—that and the scents of lavender, doughnuts, licorice, and cinnamon buns were more arousing (as measured by blood flow to the penis) than perfume.

Red dresses have often been associated with scarlet women (one piece of folk wisdom holds that it's improper to wear a red dress as a guest at a wedding because it signifies that you have slept with the groom). Brides (at least Western brides; Chinese and Indian brides often wear red) are told, "Marry in red, you'll wish yourself dead." Red dresses are also believed to attract lightning as well as men.

The right kind of red dress can make any woman (at least those at the lower end of the Kinsey scale) want to put out lures for male approval, especially if she has been denied other kinds of power.

ACCESSORIES: The Siren dress is worn with confidence, matching lipstick, high heels, and a come-hither look. What happens when they do come hither is up to you!

RELATED: The Madame X.

WORN BY: Everyone, but especially popular with ingénues seeking a more grown-up look—see Carey Mulligan, Anne Hathaway, Jennifer Lawrence, and Emma Stone, who all donned red dresses when seeking more rounded roles.

DESIGNERS: Valentino, Marchesa, Versace, Yves Saint Laurent.

THE SLIP DRESS

THE SLIP DRESS IS, in essence, just that: a slip, usually silk, worn as a dress. Traditionally, the Slip dress is bias-cut, with thin spaghetti straps, in pale colors or basic black (or, very occasionally, red), and knee length or longer.

The Slip dress balances innocence and knowingness: the innocence of a gown that could be a nightgown or negligee, exposed in a public place. The wearer of the Slip dress is pretending to be simple while being complicated: the essence of minimalism.

At its best, the Slip dress refocuses attention from the dress to the wearer: think Carolyn Bessette's Narciso Rodriguez wedding dress (and Carolyn worked for Calvin Klein, one of the early masters of the Slip dress). Even Vera Wang, the wedding dress designer, changed into a pale pink Slip dress for her own wedding reception. When worn the wrong way (too tight, too short, with overdone hair, with too much makeup, or not enough underwear) the Slip dress can be blowsy and vulgar, and occasionally the Slip dress is deliberately overclocked to make a comment about the nature of femininity (the Courtney Love).

Like the Bandage dress, the Slip dress requires confidence, but poised confidence, not mere bravado.

ACCESSORIES: Minimal (but very expensive) jewelry, high-heeled sandals with the briefest of straps, effortless hair worn down or in a simple chignon, and a tiny clutch. You can wear a shawl, but not a heavy coat, which makes the dress seem too much like lingerie.

WORN BY: Carolyn Bessette Kennedy, Cindy Crawford (who wore a Galliano version for her 1998 wedding to Rande Gerber), Alicia Silverstone as Cher in the movie *Clueless* (her dress is credited to Calvin Klein, whose design house reissued it in 2010), Angelina Jolie, Emma Watson, and, of course, Courtney Love. Honorable mention: Elizabeth Taylor in an actual slip in *Cat on a Hot Tin Roof*.

THE SPACE AGE

THE SPACE AGE DRESS is the ideal dress for your next vacation to the lunar colony or to the luxury hotels of the asteroid belt. Short, in blinding white or silvery metallic, created in some miraculous fabric that neither stains nor creases, and treated with some sort of force-field effect so that it stays put, even in zero gravity, the dress is a technological miracle in and of itself.

Of course, the true Space Age dress, the ideal one of fiction, doesn't actually exist, but a number of designers in the 1960s contributed to the overall Space Age aesthetic, especially André Courrèges, with his 1964 white-and-silver "Space Age" collection, and Pierre Cardin, in his 1966 "Cosmos" collection, which included wool shift minidresses with huge cut-outs (worn with domed felt helmets). Paco Rabanne's 1966 chain-mail-style dresses and Rudi Gernreich's 1968 dresses with transparent vinyl inserts both became classic tropes of Space Age dresses.

In the last fifty years, the Space Age dress has passed from modern to retro to classic. Wearing it conveys a sense of youthful lightheartedness and openness to possibilities (as well as a high tolerance for itchy and sticky petroleum-based fibers). It can be used to show off either an ironic design sense or exuberant nerdiness, depending on whether it's being worn at an art gallery or at a science-fiction convention. Wearing a Space Age dress says, "I think the future is going to be just fab, and I'm more than ready for it."

ACCESSORIES: Flat white midcalf boots (à la Courrèges), bug-eyed white sunglasses, tights, a phaser (set to stun; you're dressing to kill).

WORN BY: Peggy Moffitt, Audrey Hepburn, Judy Jetson, Lady Gaga, Star Trek extras.

DESIGNERS: Rudi Gernreich, André Courrèges, Paco Rabanne, Pierre Cardin, Hussein Chalayan, Oscar de la Renta.

84

SCENE: THE THRONE ROOM OF A SPACESHIP. Your boots reverberate against the hypersteel floors as you approach the dais. Seated on the transparent throne, looking as if she is floating, is the empress. The tall collar of her silvery dress frames her face and echoes the high arch of her eyebrows. The jeweled pendant of her tiara flashes with its own light from the center of her forehead. She is looking quizzically at you, her natural haughtiness warring with an unaccustomed curiosity. Her counselor raises a hand to his sidearm and ostentatiously flips it from stun to kill.

Empress: "What brings you to my realm?"

The Space Empress dress is intended to be barbarically futuristic—to awe all onlookers with the one-two punch of pageantry and science. It's usually silver in color, although the actual composition of the fabric may be anything the writers dream up, preferably involving nanotech or some other flavor of unobtainium. The Space Empress dress may have enormous shoulders or attached capes, but otherwise it features very little ornamentation. All space empresses have completely stunning physiques and waist-to-hip ratios that modern-day swimsuit models would die for, despite living in space with little fresh food and no outdoor exercise. (Also, space empresses are immune to the degenerative effects of spending time in low- or no-gravity environments.)

Space Empress dresses owe much to the art deco environment of early pulp science fiction, especially space opera.

Sometimes confused with the Space Empress dress is the Space Bikini, worn by Barbarella, Princess Leia as a slave, and Dejah Thoris (of the *John Carter of Mars* books by Edgar Rice Burroughs). Although the Space Bikini shares the future barbarism of the Space Empress dress and can have trailing (often transparent) draperies, it is usually reserved for women in need of rescuing, not women actively ruling.

ACCESSORIES: Tiaras (especially those that taper to a point on the forehead), large bejeweled cuff bracelets, disintegrating beams, lasers, large catlike creatures on golden leashes, and alternately fawning and scheming minions.

WORN BY: Space Empress dresses are rare outside of comic books, movies, and movies based on comic books, but Gwyneth Paltrow's 2012 Oscar dress (with its cape and asymmetrical neckline, designed by Tom Ford) came very close. If only she'd invested in some forehead bling . . .

THE BEST GUIDE TO THE HISTORY of the distinctive dresses worn by square dancers is a booklet put out by the United Square Dancers of America, called, forthrightly, *Square Dance Attire*. After an introduction that begins, "At this particular point in time when just about anything goes—no holds barred, it is nice to know that at a square dance there is something 'special' about the way we dress. It is special because ladies look like ladies and you don't need a program to tell the hims from the hers," we discover that what we consider to be the classic square-dancing costume, with its nods to Western style, dates back no further than square dancing's revival in the late 1930s. The big tulle petticoats that non-square-dancers find so distinctive were first made popular at square dances in the 1960s, a good decade or so after they were popular off the floor. (The booklet also devotes considerable space to proper underwear, distinguishing among pantaloons, pantalettes, pants, aloons ["what remains when the pantaloon is shortened"], panties, capris, and "sissy britches.")

The Square Dancing dress is worn not just to produce an individual effect but with an eye for how the dress will look as part of the whirl on the dance floor. Square Dancing dresses are as much for the community of dancers as they are for any one person, and dancers are exhorted to follow club, party, and convention dress codes specifically to preserve the human kaleidoscope feeling of a good square dance. Dancers know that something special would be lost if the dances became a sea of people in interchangeable outfits of T-shirts and blue jeans.

Square Dancing dresses, like gothic wear, cosplay costumes, and to a lesser extent athletic-team jerseys, loudly announce your devotion to and membership in a subculture. They say, "Yeah, I really like this, and I'm willing to wear these clothes to prove it." You wear them with your head held high, or not at all.

RELATED: The Square Dancing dress is where the Cowgirl meets the Dirndl.

THE STEAMPUNK

STEAMPUNK HAS EXPANDED from being a subgenre of science fiction, roughly defined as having a Victorian sensibility blended with anachronistic or alternative-history technology, to being more of a lifestyle aesthetic, along the lines of the goth culture. (Science-fiction writer Charlie Stross has famously said that "steampunk is nothing more than what happens when goths discover brown.")

Steampunk is a very appealing mélange of all the best parts of the various wells it draws from: the elegance and manners of the Victorian era, sepia-tone newsboy fashion, the gee-whiz high spirits of adventure and science fiction, and the intellectual appeal of human-scale technology, topped with a double scoop of maker-culture enthusiasm. The overall mood is one of fun, exploration, science, and just a little goofiness; the culture is one of experimentation, creativity, and DIY.

The idea of steampunk seems to be that the shiny silver-and-glass modern future we were promised has yet to materialize, so why don't we press the reset button and try another take? This time with more dirigibles and polished brass and fewer nuclear bombs, please.

The Steampunk dress usually features one of the following tropes: leather, tweed (or herringbone), muslin, brass, clockwork gears, grommets or rivets, pouches or belts, a bustle, a newsboy cap, a pith helmet or a top hat (I have yet to see a pith top hat, but I'm waiting), and (semi-obligatorily) goggles.

ACCESSORIES: Often worn with buckled or laced Victorian boots, frequently worn with an expression of glee.

WORN BY: Helena Bonham Carter.

DESIGNERS: Steampunk is usually DIY, but John Galliano and Alexander McQueen have been both inspired and inspirational.

THE STEWARDESS

87

BEFORE WE HAD FLIGHT ATTENDANTS laboring to keep us all safe and calm in the face of overbooked planes, overstuffed overhead bins, and $14 spotty Wi-Fi, air travel was made smoother by magical beings known as stewardesses. Stewardesses were still primarily responsible for passenger safety, of course, but in the bad old days of *Mad Men*–style male entitlement, they were also given more decorative responsibilities. A Braniff recruiting pamphlet said that "a Braniff International hostess is a beautiful person . . . a friend to everyone who boards her plane . . . She is a model in how to walk, talk, sit, stand, apply make-up properly and style her hair."

Braniff was the first airline to hire a fashion designer to create their Stewardess uniforms, tapping Emilio Pucci for the job in 1965. (Pucci also designed uniforms for Qantas, including a special perfume to go with them.) Pierre Balmain and Ralph Lauren designed uniforms for TWA, Christian Lacroix for Air France, Anne Klein for Pan American, Hanae Mori for JAL (three separate uniforms from 1967 to 1988), Mary Quant for Court Line Aviation in 1973, Giorgio Armani for Alitalia in the 1990s, Gianfranco Ferré for Korean Air (from 2005) . . . It might be difficult to find a major fashion designer who has not taken an airline commission.

It's not surprising that designers leapt at the chance to do airline uniforms. Uniforms provided the opportunity to do a complete look with hats, coats, jackets, scarves, shoes, boots, tights, sometimes even jewelry, plus the obligatory aprons or coveralls for meal service work. Designers were encouraged to be fashion-forward, with bold colors and new styles, including tunics and miniskirts. (Pacific Southwest Airlines was among the first to have hot pants as uniforms in the 1970s, a trend we shall pass over in silence.) And of course stewardesses were icons of modernism, independence, cosmopolitanism, and sex appeal, even before the appalling National Airlines campaign of the early 1970s, where attendants were compelled to wear little buttons saying "Fly me!" No better advertising could be had.

Today, flight attendant uniforms are more businesslike and passengers less grope-y (which is a good thing), and the uniforms are much more likely to be worn with union pins than with matching go-go boots. But the suggestion of adventure, sophistication, and sex appeal implied by the classic Stewardess silhouette continues to have retro appeal.

RELATED: The Airship Hostess.

WORN BY: The short-lived 2011–12 television series *Pan Am* showcased Christina Ricci as a stewardess on the famed airline.

DESIGNERS: Karl Lagerfeld (for Chanel) and Marc Jacobs (for Marc by Marc Jacobs) have both included Stewardess looks in their collections.

THE STUNT DRESS

88

WHAT'S A STUNT DRESS? It's not a dress that exists merely to draw attention, like the J-Lo, or a dress constructed as an art object or to shock (like Björk's Swan dress or the Biohazard dress). It's not a dress that requires acrobatics to get into or to wear, or special equipment (usually). A Stunt dress is one that combines something interesting or beautiful to wear with some commentary, connection, or collaboration with the event at which it's intended to be worn.

The best-known example of a Stunt dress is the dress Australian costume designer Lizzy Gardiner wore to the 1995 Academy Awards. It was constructed of 254 American Express gold credit cards. Gardiner had intended for the dress to be used in the movie *Priscilla, Queen of the Desert* (for which she won the Oscar for Best Costume Designer that year), but American Express had not given its consent. After the Oscars, American Express saw the marketing possibilities and sent the gown on a tour of its offices, and the dress was later auctioned off to benefit the American Foundation for AIDS Research. Faith Hill may or may not have been wearing an intentional Stunt dress when she wore a rainbow Versace sheath to sing "Somewhere over the Rainbow" at the 2002 Academy Awards. A more recent Stunt dress was constructed by Canadian high school student Kara Koskowich— she recycled months of her math homework to create a one-shouldered graduation dress. The fictional queen of the Stunt dress is the cartoon character Ms. Frizzle, of *Magic Schoolbus* fame: her dresses always have something to do with the day's adventure/lesson.

Personally, I love Stunt dresses and wear them all the time. I have many alphabet dresses that I wear to give talks about dictionaries, a Tetris-print dress I wore to speak at an Internet (read: nerd) conference, and crossword-puzzle-themed dresses to wear to the American Crossword Puzzle Tournament. I also have a Darth Vader–themed dress that will be a Stunt dress as soon as I find the appropriate venue for it.

ACCESSORIES: The only obligatory accessories for the Stunt dress are a strong appreciation for the absurd and a willingness to look slightly silly for a good joke or a good cause.

RELATED: The Cher, the J-Lo, the Swan.

89

IT HAD LONG SLEEVES and footless tights of spangled nude illusion netting, a knee-length poofy white tulle skirt . . . and a bodice shaped to look like the head and neck of a swan, wrapped around Björk's own neck. The infamous Swan dress, which the Icelandic singer wore to the 2001 Academy Awards, is unforgettable.

In addition to wearing the dress, designed by her friend and sometime collaborator Marjan Pejoski, Björk brought six eggs with her and dropped them along the red carpet as she went, causing even more consternation. (In an interview with *Spin* magazine, Björk said that other stars' bodyguards kept telling her, "Sorry, ma'am, you dropped this.") In other interviews, Björk has talked about her "obsession" with swans—to her they symbolize winter, romance, and monogamy, among other things, and she's worn versions of the swan dress for live shows and on the cover of her album *Vespertine*.

Not everyone can wear an actual Swan dress, although Ellen DeGeneres, Kevin James, and Miley Cyrus (in character as Hannah Montana) have all worn parodic versions. The idea of a Swan dress—a dress that you wear to add a note of absurdity or surreality, or just to be true to your own aesthetic ideals and obsessions—is one that can be carried out to completion by anyone brave and creative enough to do so.

ACCESSORIES: Björk wore her Swan dress with Balenciaga heels and a sense of playfulness; the designer shoes are optional, but the playfulness is not.

RELATED: The Cher, the Stunt dress.

THE T-SHIRT DRESS

90

THE T-SHIRT AS WE KNOW IT began as institutionalized underwear—first as part of navy uniforms, and then as part of the uniforms of all branches of the service. After World War II, the T-shirt moved into civilian life with the returning soldiers and became a familiar item. The T-Shirt dress began its long reign of popularity in the 1950s, with a fashion feature in *Life* in 1954 proclaiming that "the dress is comfortable, washable, and a whole wardrobe of them can be stacked without crushing in a bureau drawer . . . [and] can be had for little more than the price of a child's T-shirt."

The T-Shirt dress comes in almost as many varieties as the T-shirt itself: tight and loose, white, black, and every color in between, screen-printed and logoed, striped and solid, mini-length and ankle-grazing. The T-Shirt dress has all the virtues of the T-shirt: comfort, ease of wear, and a varying degree of body-consciousness, depending on the preferences of the wearer.

The T-Shirt dress is probably the lowest common denominator of American sportswear—wearable by almost anyone, at almost any time, with minimal adjustments due to time of day and venue. (There even probably exists a T-Shirt dress with an evening gown printed on the front, to be worn as partner to the tuxedo-print T-shirt.) A T-Shirt dress seems to promise a permanent state of sunny Saturday afternoon picnic hopping, with a bike ride, a cookout, and a quick trip around the lake in a boat to boot.

ACCESSORIES: The T-Shirt dress is best worn with either no belt at all or a very casual one (a scarf, a bandanna, or one of canvas or woven leather), sneakers or flat sandals, and minimal jewelry (or, for the 1980s-revival look, big plastic beads). A bathing suit underneath is optional but highly recommended.

RELATED: The Shirtdress, the Polo dress, the Is-It-a-Shirt?, the Mary Quant, the Face.

DESIGNERS: The Gap, Ralph Lauren, Tommy Hilfiger.

THE TENNIS DRESS

91

IN THE EARLY DAYS OF TENNIS (or "lawn tennis," to distinguish it from "real tennis," a complicated and archaic game played on something resembling a squash court) players wore their own ordinary clothes, including hats, with women perhaps wearing a tennis pinafore or apron with pockets for extra balls. Tennis player Violet Sutton, the sister of May Sutton, the first American woman to win at Wimbledon, reminisced in 1972 about the clothes they had to wear to play: "A long undershirt, pair of drawers, two petticoats, white linen corset cover, duck shirt [a stiff canvas corsetlike bodice], shirtwaist, long white silk stockings, and a floppy hat." White was favored for tennis wear because it hid the signs of sweating—and who wouldn't sweat wearing all that?

The increasing involvement of women in sports led to more demand for sports-specific clothing, especially for golf and tennis. Jean Patou was one of the early designers who made sleeveless tennis dresses with shorter skirts; one of his dresses was worn at Wimbledon in 1919. (Although as the dresses got shorter and play became more athletic, girls were advised to wear two pairs of tennis knickers, one over the other, just in case.)

The classic short tennis dress, with its sleeveless bodice, short pleated skirt, and matching underwear, is the counterargument to all the stuffy naysayers who predicted that tennis would "thicken the ankles, coarsen the complexion, and lead to general ungainliness" of the women who played it (from a British *Vogue* editorial, crowing that for British girls at least, that fear was unfounded). Over time, sports (and sports clothes) have become more unisex, with the exception of the tennis dress. There's no obligation to be traditionally feminine while playing any sport, of course, but there's also no prohibition against it, and the tennis dress proves that it's entirely possible to have a pretty outfit and a pretty mean serve simultaneously.

ACCESSORIES: The tennis dress is best worn with a killer backhand. It's also a good excuse to indulge in socks with pom-poms.

DESIGNERS: Teddy Tinling, Venus Williams.

THE TIMES SQUARE **92**

THE TIMES SQUARE DRESS is any dress that lights up. Whether powered by batteries, the wearer's kinetic energy, solar power, or (someday) nuclear fusion, a dress that glows of its own accord always gathers fascinated attention.

Times Square dresses used to be for conceptual artists and MIT students only, but recent advances in electronics (especially the easy-to-use LilyPad Arduino controllers) and the rise of maker culture have opened up new horizons and new possibilities. A couple of LEDs, a few watch batteries, a little soldering, and you too can glow in the dark, flash scrolling messages, or twinkle like a Christmas tree, and what could be more fun than that?

The Times Square dress is part fashion, part art, and part prize-winning science project; more than half the fun of a good Times Square dress is in the planning and construction. A true Times Square dress is one-of-a-kind, handmade, and built as much for proving that it can be done as for eventual wearing.

ACCESSORIES: A feeling of accomplishment, a step-by-step set of instructions posted on your blog, and the heady perfume of fresh solder. Whether worn to your local Arduino hacker meetup or to the Metropolitan Museum of Art's Costume Gala (as singer Katy Perry did in 2010), the Times Square dress is well worth whatever it costs in engineering effort and batteries.

RELATED: The Stunt dress, the Biohazard.

DESIGNERS: Diana Eng (of *Project Runway* fame), Hussein Chalayan.

THE *TITANIC*

93

THE 1997 JAMES CAMERON MOVIE epic *Titanic* had a budget of more than $200 million, a hit song (the inescapable "My Heart Will Go On," sung by Céline Dion), a catchphrase ("I'm the king of the world!"), and the top spot as the highest-grossing movie of all time for twelve years. It was nominated for fourteen Academy Awards and won eleven, including Best Picture, Best Director, and (most relevant for our purposes) Best Costume Design.

The dresses in *Titanic* were (as suited the story) elegant Edwardian creations, befitting first-class passengers of the Gilded Age. But obviously an epic love story needs an epic dress, and one dress in particular—in which Rose (played by Kate Winslet) stands like a figurehead at the prow of the great doomed ship—has taken on iconic-movie-dress status. You can buy reproductions online for your prom (or, for your wedding, the version in white that was—spoiler alert!—shown at the end of the movie). A replica, including a matching evening bag, was available for a while from the J. Peterman catalog.

The *Titanic* dress is just an extreme example of the totemic nature of clothing—we see someone we admire wearing something we otherwise wouldn't spare two thoughts for (bedazzled flip-flops? outré sunglasses? suspenders?), and suddenly we find ourselves looking for the styling credits or running to Google. At some primitive level, we think that sharing what some paragon is wearing will lead to our sharing that person's other qualities, too, and that goes double for fictional characters, for whom every detail has been carefully selected. Of course the *Titanic* dress stands for eternal love—it was specifically designed to!

ACCESSORIES: The *Titanic* dress is worn with "My Heart Will Go On" blasting in the background and a poster of Leonardo DiCaprio on your bedroom wall.

DESIGNER: Costume designer Deborah L. Scott.

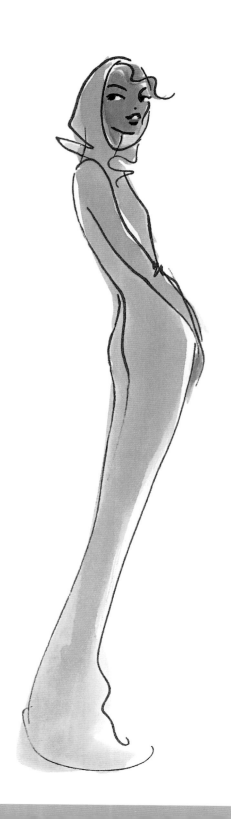

THE TURTLENECK-HOODED COWL DRESS

94

THERE IS NO EARTHLY REASON for this dress to exist, other than that, against all odds, it looks cool. A long tube, so long that the top extends over the head, with long sleeves? It's like wearing a giant sock, if giant socks were made in silver Lurex. Despite being hard to move in (either because it's a long tight column or because it has a drapey hood that has to be positioned just so), obstructing your vision (that hood), and being unforgiving of less-than-perfect figures (that long tight column thing again), the Turtleneck-Hooded Cowl Dress (or THCD for short) works by focusing all attention on your face. (Which is why, in fashion magazine editorials, this dress is almost always shot from the shoulders up.) The THCD can make almost anyone look like the mysterious female lead in a science-fiction movie.

There's no point in accessorizing anything below the neck with the THCD, because how do you accessorize a knit shroud? You only have to worry about your face: add as many false eyelashes as you can manage, and maybe big hoop earrings. You might as well wear comfy shoes, though, since they won't be noticed (although heavy boots, such as Doc Martens or combat boots, are a nice apocalyptic touch). And it's a good thing you're in a science-fiction movie, because there's no place to put pockets on the THCD. (You have to put your lip gloss and ID in a tiny interdimensional portal that you open by whistling).

WORN BY: Grace Jones, Bianca Jagger, Liza Minnelli, Rihanna, Amber Rose, Lindsay Lohan.

DESIGNERS: Alexander McQueen, Halston, Azzedine Alaïa, Thierry Mugler, Brian Lichtenberg.

95

THE VIONNET

THE VIONNET DRESS is a puzzle in three-dimensional space: a three-body problem, with the three bodies being your body, the bias-cut fabric of the dress, and the space through which both of you move.

Madame Vionnet began working as an apprentice to a dressmaker when she was very young, and moved to Paris at the turn of the last century to work for Callot Soeurs, a renowned couture house. It was there that she began to practice draping, building garments on a miniature dress form instead of as flat pattern pieces. Inspired by such avant-garde figures as Isadora Duncan, Vionnet started working on her own daring designs in 1907 at the house of Doucet, although they were worn not in public but in the privacy of the tea hour at home. (Perhaps for the "four-to-five," the understood time for infidelity in France, during which loose and informal "déshabillé" dress was accepted, and tight corsets would have been a serious inconvenience.) Vionnet opened her own design house in 1912, but it was not until after World War I that she began making the bias-cut dresses that are her legacy. Vionnet continued experimenting with fabric, including new dyeing methods and precisely engineered pintucks, until she showed her last collection in 1939.

ACCESSORIES: Your own graceful motion (if you aren't naturally graceful, a Vionnet dress will make you so) and the play of light over the fabric. The worst thing you can do is hold still, caging the potential of the dress.

WORN BY: Marlene Dietrich, Joan Crawford.

96

DIANA VREELAND (1903–1989) was the editor of *Vogue* for nearly ten years; she spent more than twenty years before that at *Harper's Bazaar* and was the creative director for more than a dozen landmark exhibitions at the Costume Institute of the Metropolitan Museum of Art from the early 1970s through the mid-1980s.

Her groundbreaking editorial work helped launch many careers, including those of models Veruschka and Twiggy and designers Diane von Furstenberg and Oscar de la Renta; she was one of the first to print models' names in fashion spreads. She was also famous for her gnomic pronouncements, at first from her "Why Don't You?" column for *Harper's Bazaar* ("Why don't you . . . have a yellow satin bed entirely quilted in butterflies" is one example), but also such widely quoted statements as "Pink is the navy blue of India" and "Elegance is refusal." Her own style was meticulous—she once said, "Unshined shoes are the end of civilization"—and striking, with deep black hair, Chinese-red nail polish, and intense red rouge on her cheeks, forehead, and earlobes. (She also said, "Exaggeration is my only reality.")

One of Vreeland's "Why Don't You?" questions was "Why don't you . . . find one dress that you like and have it copied many times? You will be much more successful than if you try to produce new effects each evening." The Vreeland dress is the dress that strikes you in this way—so flattering, so easy to wear, simple enough to reproduce, but complex enough to support multiple iterations. Vreeland was able to have Balenciaga make hers; the rest of us are not so lucky.

As Vreeland said, "Everything is interpretation." (Even Vreeland's given name was up for interpretation: a *Vanity Fair* article in 1993 pointed out that even her close friends said it variously as "dee-AH-nah," "die-ANN-uh," or "dee-AHN.") The trick, as Vreeland knew, is in finding the right source material to interpret.

RELATED: The Chanel Jersey dress, the Mouret.

THE WENCH 97

THE CLASSIC WENCH DRESS is the one we all recognize from costume parties and period dramas: the off-the-shoulder bodice, the impossibly tiny, corseted waist, and the full swishing skirt. The wench is equally comfortable serving beer and fighting off pirates (or maybe running off to join them), and knows to the ounce and the minute when a drunken customer will save her the trouble of concussing him by passing out on his own.

Although the Wench dress seems archaic, the concept embodied by the Wench dress—an attractive woman serving up alcohol, cheerfulness, and the unfulfilled promise of sexual availability—has persisted through the ages (see the Stewardess). It is alive and well in those establishments that are collectively called "breastaurants" and which outfit their staff in tight tees and tiny shorts instead of low-cut bodices and swirling skirts.

Wench dresses are popular at Oktoberfests, where they compete with the Dirndl, becoming more prevalent the farther you get from Austria, and Renaissance Faires, where they are more fun to wear than the Guinevere, and, of course, at various pirate-themed gatherings.

ACCESSORIES: A brimming foamy mug of beer, an extra hand for dealing with gropers, and the knowledge that serving beer is a very difficult way to make a living. (Add a sword for pirate wenches.)

RELATED: The Stewardess, the Dirndl, the Xena.

WORN BY: Kim Kardashian (as a Halloween costume, but still . . .)

DESIGNERS: Jean Paul Gaultier; Alexander McQueen and Vivienne Westwood have cited pirates as themes or inspirations.

98

EVERYTHING THERE IS TO KNOW and love about 1930s screen siren fashion is available in the 1939 film *The Women*, directed by George Cukor. The movie even includes a ten-minute-long fashion show of designs—playsuits! evening gowns! women in hats feeding monkeys (also in hats)! and all in Technicolor!—by Adrian, the leading movie costume designer of the day.

White fur and marabou, sparkling sequins and shiny lamé, chiffon and charmeuse, big shoulders and little hats (and turbans!)—Norma Shearer, Rosalind Russell, and Joan Crawford wear them all. The reason we love 1930s movie fashion so much, though, is because it was designed—engineered, really—to be pure escapism. Worried or distraught? Focus instead on a long white column of shimmering satin, reflecting and retaining the moonlight on the terrace, where some debonair man may soon appear to say some witty things. There is no better distraction to be had, on or off the screen. The gowns were just as expressive as the actresses who wore them (and in some cases appeared higher in the credits).

If you can pull one off today (it helps to be tall and slender, and to have an assistant available to follow you around with a steamer so that your satin never shows creases), remember that the classic 1930s screen idol dress is worn with a permanent wave, Jungle Red fingernail polish, and ever so slightly more diamonds than are strictly necessary.

RELATED: The Siren, the First Oscar.

WORN BY: Gwen Stefani, Gwyneth Paltrow, Drew Barrymore.

DESIGNERS: John Galliano (for Dior), Junya Watanabe, Zac Posen.

THE WRAP DRESS

"FEEL LIKE A WOMAN, WEAR A DRESS" was the tagline Diane von Furstenberg used for her classic 1970s knit jersey Wrap dress. The first Wrap dress (in a wood-grain print) appeared in 1972 and was an instant success. At its peak in 1975, fifteen thousand Wrap dresses were sold each week, and the dress was featured on the cover of *Newsweek* and on the front page of the *Wall Street Journal.*

Revived in 1997, the dress again sold in the millions. A fashionable, flattering, comfortable, washable, adjustable dress (you never have a "fat day" in a Wrap dress) will always have a place in women's closets—there's even one in the Smithsonian Institution.

But the reason the Wrap dress is so popular with working women is because Diane von Furstenberg (despite being a real-life princess from her first marriage) is a working woman herself. She apprenticed at the factories that made her dresses and learned the business there; she dragged her own sample cases around to department stores; she appeared in her own ads. And when she made her comeback in the early 1990s, she went on QVC and sold more than a million dollars' worth of merchandise in less than two hours. The Wrap dress is what working women wanted, and Diane von Furstenberg wanted it, too.

ACCESSORIES: Loafers, low heels, or knee-high boots; big sunglasses; great jewelry; a slouchy bag; and occasionally (depending on the windiness of the day) a few strategically placed safety pins.

RELATED: The Chanel Jersey dress, the Mouret.

WORN BY: Diane von Furstenberg's memoir lists Candice Bergen, Cybill Shepherd, Mary Tyler Moore, Betty Ford, Angela Davis, Gloria Steinem, and Cheryl Tiegs as all having worn the Wrap in its early heyday.

XENA, THE TITLE CHARACTER in the television series *Xena: Warrior Princess* (1995–2001), is a former warlord and outlaw on a quest to redeem her violent past. To do this, of course, she still needs to do a lot of fighting . . . just for the right things this time. She wears an armored leather bustier connected to a short leather segmented skirt, armbands, gauntlets, shoulder pieces, and boots.

The Xena dress is a vast improvement over the general run of sword-fantasy costumes for women, which often seem to be collected under the heading "decorative cast-iron underwear." Xena's costume is still revealing and on the breast-centric side, but it's designed for fighting, not for being rescued—a huge improvement. (Besides, it looks great, and this is cable television, after all.) Xena is feminine but kick-ass: as comic book artist and editor Sarah Dyer put it, "She proves you can fight really good in a skirt."

The Xena is not exactly street wear (unless a comics convention is happening on your street), but it's still a favorite Halloween costume, and faithful replicas can sell for close to a thousand dollars online.

Ngila Dickson, the costume designer, won the Best Contribution to Design award for the Xena from New Zealand Television in 1996 and 1997, and Lucy Lawless, who played Xena, donated her costume to the National Museum of American History in 2006.

ACCESSORIES: A sword, laced boots or gladiator sandals, and complete disregard for the opinions of people who don't enjoy strong female characters.

RELATED: The Wench, the Dirndl.

DESIGNERS: The full-on Xena look is a little over the top, even for couture, but Kate and Laura Mulleavy of Rodarte included a very Xenaesque gold leather gladiator dress in their spring 2011 collection.

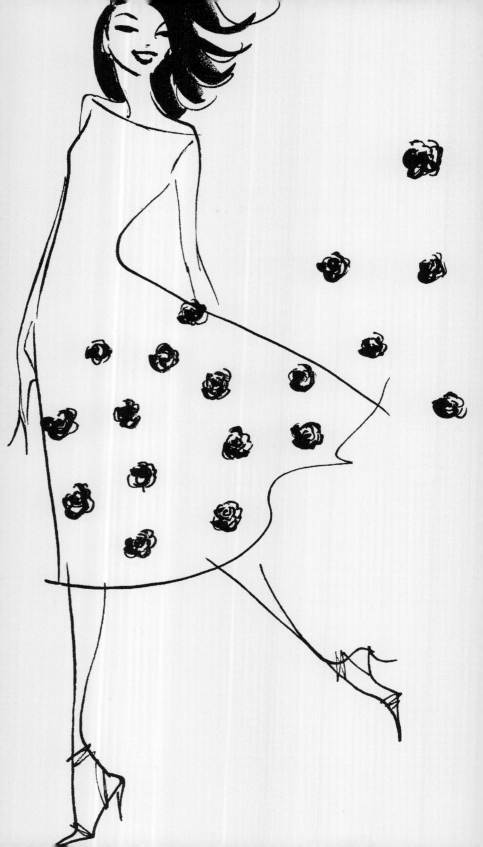

Acknowledgments

Many, many thanks to Donna Mehalko, who, in our talks together, managed to take a rather hapless collection of random adjectives and inchoate gesturing and turn them into actual images with pinpoint accuracy. I am forever grateful for your patience, good humor, helpful suggestions, and sense of fun!

Thanks also to the intrepid souls who volunteered to beta-read this book: Connie Baboukis, Erin Black, Elizabeth Brewer, Kathleen Cooper, Skye Forster, Erica Goebel, Inez Gowsell, Heather Schechter, Lee Smith, Emily Star, and Susan Welstead. Thank you for putting up with my tendency to insert semicolons where commas have rightful tenancy, and also for rescuing me from far too many embarrassing errors (and parenthetical expressions). Any errors (and parenthetical expressions) that remain, of course, are solely my own responsibility.

This book would not be in your hands without the intercessions of Lisa Bankoff, my extremely patient agent; the guiding care of Nancy Miller, who, if she were a fictional editor, would be met by accusations of authorial wish fulfillment; and the tolerant ear of my sister Kate McKean. Thanks also to my wonderful co-workers at Wordnik, who patiently indulge my not-so-hidden life as a dress junkie.

And, as always, my love and thanks to Joey and Henry Gerharz, who, in addition to leaving me time to write, have mastered the art of at least *seeming* to be interested in dresses.

One Hundred Books About Dresses

100 DRESSES: THE COSTUME INSTITUTE
Harold Koda (Yale University Press, 2010).
*Shows off dresses from the permanent
collection of the Metropolitan Museum of
Art, especially famous dresses such as the
Duchess of Windsor's wedding dress.*

100 YEARS OF FASHION ILLUSTRATION
Cally Blackman (Laurence King Publishers,
2007). *Great reference book for both
illustrators and illustration junkies.*

400 YEARS OF FASHION
Natalie Rothstein (V&A,
2010). *A treasure trove
from the V&A's collection,
covering accessories as
well as dresses.*

**ADRIAN: SILVER SCREEN TO
CUSTOM LABEL**
Christian Esquevin
(Monacelli Press, 2008).
*Covers Adrian's movie
costumes as well as his
work for private clients
and his own label.*

ADVANCED STYLE
Ari Seth Cohen (Powerhouse Books, 2010).
*Wonderful collection of photographs
(inspired by the author's blog) featuring
chic and stylish women over sixty.*

ALEXANDER MCQUEEN: SAVAGE BEAUTY
Andrew Bolton et al. (Metropolitan Museum
of Art, 2011). *The book accompaniment to
the landmark 2011 exhibition.*

ALLURE
Diana Vreeland (Chronicle, 2010).
*This reprinted edition is smaller and
condensed from the original, but still
packed full of Vreelandisms ("Really,
we should forget all this nonsense and
just stay home and read Proust").*

ALWAYS IN VOGUE
Edna Woolman and Ilka Chase (Gollancz,
1954). *The autobiography of the former
editor of Vogue (1914–1952), Edna
Woolman Chase.*

AMERICAN FASHION
Charlie Scheips (Assouline, 2007).
*American fashion from the 1920s through
the early twenty-first century.*

**ANGLOMANIA: TRADITION AND TRANSGRESSION IN
BRITISH FASHION**
Andrew Bolton et al. (Metropolitan Museum
of Art, 2007). *The companion volume to the
glorious show of the same name at the Met.*

ART DECO FASHION
Suzanne Lussier (Bullfinch, 2003).
*Beautifully illustrated book on the
intersection of Art Deco and clothes.*

AVEDON FASHION 1944–2000
Carol Squiers et al. (Abrams, 2009). *Images
from Avedon's long career, accompanying
the Avedon exhibit at International Center
of Photography in May 2009.*

BALENCIAGA
Pierre Arizzoli-Clémentel, Miren Arzalluz,
and Amalia Descalzo (Thames and Hudson,
2011). *Published to accompany the opening
of the Balenciaga Museum in Spain, with
more than five hundred gorgeous illustrations of the designer's work.*

**THE BEAUTIFUL FALL: FASHION, GENIUS, AND GLORIOUS
EXCESS IN 1970S PARIS**
Alicia Drake (Hachette, 2007). *Yves Saint
Laurent, Karl Lagerfeld, and 1970s Paris—
what more could you want?*

THE BERG COMPANION TO FASHION
Valerie Steele (Berg, 2010). *With articles on
everything from Afros to zoot suits, a handy
and compact overview of fashion trends
and topics.*

**BEST DRESSED: FASHION FROM THE BIRTH OF COUTURE
TO TODAY**
Dilys E. Blum (Philadelphia Museum of Art,
1997). *Highlights from the costume collection at the Philadelphia Museum of Art,
including dresses by Charles Worth.*

BETTER THAN BEAUTY: A GUIDE TO CHARM
Helen Valentine and Alice Thompson
(Chronicle, 2002). *A reprint of the 1938
guide, including such timeless advice as
"Be kind to saleswomen" and "Use a good-
quality lipstick."*

THE BLACK DRESS
Valerie Steele (HarperCollins, 2007). *An
extended meditation on the black dress,
little or big, and the role that color has
played in fashion.*

CELIA BIRTWELL
Celia Birtwell (St. Martin's Press, 2011). *A personal and in-depth look at Celia Birtwell's life and work.*

CHANEL: COLLECTIONS AND CREATIONS
Danièle Bott (Thames and Hudson, 2007). *A look at the Chanel legacy via the tropes of the house: the suit, the camellia, the perfumes, jewelry and makeup, and the little black dress.*

THE CLASSIC TEN: THE TRUE STORY OF THE LITTLE BLACK DRESS AND NINE OTHER FASHION FAVORITES
Nancy MacDonell Smith (Penguin, 2003). *Covers not only the "little black dress" but also the white shirt, the cashmere sweater, blue jeans, the suit, high heels, and the trench coat, among others.*

COSTUME DESIGN IN THE MOVIES: AN ILLUSTRATED GUIDE TO THE WORK OF 157 GREAT DESIGNERS
Elizabeth Leese (Dover, 1991). *Comprehensive guide to costume designers, with index of six thousand movies.*

COUTURE, THE GREAT DESIGNERS
Caroline Rennolds Milbank (Stewart Tabori & Chang). *Another book of eye candy, including dresses by Pauline Trigère, Kenzo, and Perry Ellis.*

THE CULTURE OF FASHION: A NEW HISTORY OF FASHIONABLE DRESS
Christopher Breward (Manchester University Press, 1995). *Has more of a focus on men's fashion and gender politics than most fashion histories; ranges from the Middle Ages to the modern day.*

THE CUTTING EDGE: 50 YEARS OF BRITISH FASHION
Amy de la Haye (Overlook Press, 1997). *Covers everyone from Hardy Amies to Vivienne Westwood, with plenty of photographs.*

DAPHNE GUINNESS
Valerie Steele (Yale University Press, 2011). *The companion volume to the Fashion Institute of Technology's exhibition on her stunning wardrobe.*

DIANA VREELAND: THE EYE HAS TO TRAVEL
Lisa Immordino Vreeland (Abrams, 2011). *A visual exploration of Vreeland's influence on fashion journalism.*

DIANE VON FURSTENBERG: THE WRAP
André Leon Talley (Assouline, 2004). *The Vogue correspondent examines the famous dress.*

DIANE: A SIGNATURE LIFE
Diane von Furstenberg and Linda Bird Francke (Simon and Schuster, 1998). *Diane von Furstenberg's fascinating memoir.*

A DICTIONARY OF COSTUME AND FASHION: HISTORIC AND MODERN
Mary Brooks Picken (Dover Editions, 1998). *Reprint editions of this classic are widely available, with more than ten thousand terms defined and more than 750 illustrations.*

THE DICTIONARY OF FASHION HISTORY
Valerie Cumming, C. W. Cunnington, and P. E. Cunnington (Berg, 2010). *An update of the landmark* Dictionary of English Costume, *enlarged by Valerie Cumming, the chair of the Costume Society. Perfect for figuring out what a "Ranelagh mob" or "loon pants" are.*

DIOR
Alexandra Palmer (V&A Publishing, 2009). *A comprehensive look at Christian Dior and the business of Dior, covering 1947–1957.*

DIOR BY DIOR
Christian Dior (V&A Museum, 2007). *The designer's autobiography.*

THE DRESS DOCTOR: PRESCRIPTIONS FOR STYLE, FROM A TO Z
Edith Head (HarperCollins, 2008). *A reprint of the 1959 edition of Edith Head's best-selling memoir and style guide, including tips on style and Hollywood anecdotes.*

ECCENTRIC GLAMOUR: CREATING AN INSANELY MORE FABULOUS YOU
Simon Doonan (Simon & Schuster, 2008). *A book intended to serve as "an antidote to the epidemic of slutty dressing and porno-chic." It's hilarious to boot.*

EDITH HEAD: THE FIFTY-YEAR CAREER OF HOLLYWOOD'S GREATEST COSTUME DESIGNER
Jay Jorgensen (Running Press, 2010). *Includes sketches, test shots, and other materials from the designer's own archives.*

ELEGANCE
Genevieve Antoine Dariaux (Doubleday, 1964). *Advice—and lots of it—from the former directrice of Nina Ricci, including "A wool suit should never be accompanied by very dressy shoes such as satin pumps or even low-cut calf pumps with slender high heels," "It is not at all chic to advertise your monogram—or, even worse, your first name—in a pin or clip, even if it is written in letters of solid gold," and "The mink cape-stole has become so banal that it can absolutely no longer figure in the wardrobe of an elegant woman."*

THE ENGLISHNESS OF ENGLISH DRESS
Christopher Breward, Becky Conekin, and Caroline Cox (Berg, 2002). *An investigation of what makes fashion English, from the eighteenth to the twenty-first centuries.*

FABULOUS FROCKS
Jane Eastoe and Sarah Gristwood (Pavilion, 2009). *Thematic chapters about twentieth-century dresses (themes include the feminine, sex, must-haves, fantasy, classical, and art), in a straightforward style.*

FASHION
Akiko Fukai et al. (The Kyoto Costume Institute) (Taschen, 2007). *Gorgeous two-volume collection of fashion history, covering the eighteenth through the twentieth centuries, drawing on the archives of the Kyoto Costume Institute.*

FASHION—PHILOSOPHY FOR EVERYONE: THINKING WITH STYLE
Fritz Allhoff, Jeanette Kennett, Jessica Wolfendale, and Jennifer Baumgardner (John Wiley & Sons, 2011). *Very thinky book—if you like your dresses with a side of Kant, this is the book for you.*

FASHION IN FICTION: TEXT AND CLOTHING IN LITERATURE, FILM AND TELEVISION
Peter McNeil, Vicki Karaminas, and Cathy Cole (Berg, 2009). *Academic essays on the role of clothes in fictional narratives, including film, television, and advertising.*

FASHION IS SPINACH
Elizabeth Hawes (Random House, 1938). *Hard to find, but a classic. Hawes argues for style over fashion, and convincingly persuades.*

FASHION, ITALIAN STYLE
Valerie Steele (Yale University Press, 2003). *Italian fashion since 1945, including the business of Italian fashion.*

FASHION: 150 YEARS OF COUTURIERS, DESIGNERS, LABELS
Charlotte Seeling (Ullmann, 2010). *Fantastic reference book—very comprehensive.*

FASHION: THE TWENTIETH CENTURY
François Baudot (Universe, 2006). *Covers eras, designers, and trends.*

THE FASHION READER (2ND ED.)
Linda Welters and Abby Lillethun (Berg, 2011). *A key fashion textbook/anthology. Read this and skip going to fashion school.*

FASHIONING SOCIETY: A HUNDRED YEARS OF HAUTE COUTURE BY SIX DESIGNERS
Karl Aspelund (Fairchild, 2009). *An academic look at the history of haute couture, from the late 1800s to the 1970s.*

FIFTY DRESSES THAT CHANGED THE WORLD
London's Design Museum (Conran, 2009). *Also features Wallis Simpson's wedding dress, alongside Alexander McQueen's "Samurai" dress of 2001. Geared toward fashion insiders.*

FIFTY YEARS OF FASHION: NEW LOOK TO NOW
Valerie Steele (Yale University Press, 2000). *From the New Look to the gray-flannel-suit era to the swinging sixties and beyond.*

THE GLASS OF FASHION
Cecil Beaton (Cassell, 1989). *Beaton's personal take (personally illustrated) on fashion in the first half of the twentieth century.*

THE GOLDEN AGE OF COUTURE: PARIS AND LONDON 1947-1957
Claire Wilcox (V&A Publishing, 2009). *Covers ten years of the most beautiful, feminine, and fun dresses ever made.*

THE GREAT FASHION DESIGNERS
Brenda Polan and Roger Tredre (Berg, 2009). *In-depth looks (including interviews) with fifty of the world's most prominent fashion designers.*

HARPER'S BAZAAR: GREATEST HITS
Glenda Bailey and Stephen Gan (Abrams, 2011). *Three hundred of the most iconic photographs from Harper's Bazaar.*

HIGH STYLE: MASTERWORKS FROM THE BROOKLYN MUSEUM COSTUME COLLECTION AT THE METROPOLITAN MUSEUM OF ART
Jan Reeder (Metropolitan Museum of Art, 2010). *Wonderful pictures of garments from the Brooklyn Museum collection— many of which have never or rarely been exhibited before.*

THE HUNDRED DRESSES
Eleanor Estes (Harcourt Brace, 1944). *The classic children's book.*

HUSSEIN CHALAYAN
Hussein Chalayan et al. (Rizzoli, 2011). *The designer's take on his body of work to date.*

IN STYLE: CELEBRATING FIFTY YEARS OF THE COSTUME INSTITUTE
Jean L. Druesdow (Metropolitan Museum of Art, 1987). *Gorgeous color photographs of classic dresses from the Met's collection.*

IN THE MOOD FOR CHEONGSAM: A SOCIAL HISTORY, 1920S-PRESENT
The National Museum of Singapore (Didier Millet, 2012). *A comprehensive history of the iconic dress, with an especial focus on its history in Singapore.*

IN VOGUE: THE ILLUSTRATED HISTORY OF THE WORLD'S MOST FAMOUS FASHION MAGAZINE
Albert Oliva and Norberto Angeletti (Rizzoli, 2006). *From its society-journal beginnings to the current Wintour era, a comprehensive account of the world's most famous fashion magazine.*

ISABELLA BLOW: A LIFE IN FASHION
Lauren Goldstein Crowe (Macmillan, 2010). *A biography of fashion legend Isabella Blow.*

IT'S SO YOU: 35 WOMEN WRITE ABOUT PERSONAL EXPRESSION THROUGH FASHION AND STYLE
Michelle Tea (Seal Press, 2007). *How do you find your own style without selling out? With essays from Sonic Youth's Kim Gordon, model Jenny Shimizu, and producer Jill Soloway, among others.*

JACQUES FATH
Jeromine Savignon (Assouline, 2009). *A collection of work by the irreverent designer, focusing on his 1950s peak.*

LANVIN
Dean Merceron (Rizzoli, 2007). *An overview of the house of Lanvin, with a focus on the collections from 1909 through 1946.*

LITTLE BLACK DRESS: VINTAGE TREASURE
Didier Ludot (Assouline, 2001). *A collection of timeless little black dresses from the proprietor of Le Petit Robe Noir in Paris.*

LOVE, LOSS, AND WHAT I WORE
Ilene Beckerman (Algonquin, 2005). *The classic book on what we feel when we remember what we wore.*

MADAME GRÈS: SPHINX OF FASHION
Patricia Mears (Yale, 2008). *Overview of Madame Grès and her long career.*

MADELEINE VIONNET
Betty Kirke (Chronicle, 1998). *Includes more than four hundred illustrations and more than thirty-five patterns for Vionnet dresses.*

A MATTER OF STYLE: HOW 10 FAMOUS WOMEN CHANGED FASHION
Paola Saltari (White Star Publishers, 2010). *Coco Chanel, Katharine Hepburn, Grace Kelly, Audrey Hepburn, Brigitte Bardot, Marilyn Monroe, Jacqueline Kennedy, Mary Quant, Twiggy, Lady Diana, and their long-lasting effect on fashion.*

MY FAVOURITE DRESS
Gity Monsef, Samantha Erin Safer, and Robert de Niet (Antique Collector's Club, 2009). *Designers, models, and fashionistas (and Kylie Minogue) discuss their favorite dresses. An expansion of the 2003 show at the Fashion and Textile Museum in London.*

MY MOTHER'S WEDDING DRESS: THE LIFE AND AFTERLIFE OF CLOTHES
Justine Picardie (Bloomsbury, 2005). *A series of thoughtful essays on the roles clothes play in our lives, whether we acknowledge them or not.*

NEW LOOK TO NOW: FRENCH HAUTE COUTURE
Stephen de Pietri and Melissa Leventon (Fine Arts Museum San Francisco, 1989). *History of French fashion from World War II to the late 1980s.*

OBSESSED BY DRESS
Tobi Tobias (Beacon, 2000). *A collection of apt and intriguing quotations on fashion and the fashionable, with such gems as: "Clothes are . . . nothing less than the furniture of the mind made visible" (James Laver) and "The intoxicating aspect of bad taste lies in the aristocratic pleasure of giving offense" (Baudelaire).*

THE ONE HUNDRED: A GUIDE TO THE PIECES EVERY STYLISH WOMAN MUST OWN
Nina Garcia (HarperCollins, 2010). *Fashion director Nina Garcia lists the hundred items that make the core of her wardrobe, including Converse sneakers, a cape, and the BlackBerry.*

OPULENT ERA: FASHIONS OF WORTH, DOUCET AND PINGAT
Elizabeth Ann Coleman (Thames & Hudson, 1989). *A gorgeous look at French fashions from the nineteenth century.*

OSSIE CLARK 1965-1974
Judith Watt (V&A Museum, 2006). *Biography of the groundbreaking British designer, with new photographs and previously unpublished sketches.*

PARIS FASHION: A CULTURAL HISTORY
Valerie Steele (Berg, 1998). *A history of Paris fashion and haute couture, and their influence on the world beyond France.*

PARISIAN CHIC: A STYLE GUIDE BY INÈS DE LA FRESSANGE
Inès de la Fressange (Flammarion, 2011). *The famous model/muse shares her tips (mostly about where to shop) for living (and looking) like a famous model/muse.*

THE PARTY DRESS BOOK: HOW TO SEW THE BEST DRESS IN THE ROOM
Mary Adams (Potter Craft, 2010). *Get inspired and make your own fabulous dress!*

PIERRE CARDIN
Elisabeth Langle (Vendome, 2005). *The first man who wanted to be a brand and not just a label.*

POIRET
Harold Koda (Metropolitan Museum of Art, 2007). *Definitive volume about the designer, including new photographs of his creations.*

PRADA
Michael Rock et al. (Abrams, 2010). *Includes an overview of all the designer's collections, and details about the innovative architecture of the brand's stores, as well as all the shoes, bags, and accessories Prada is famous for.*

RADICAL BY DESIGN: THE LIFE AND STYLE OF ELIZABETH HAWES
Bettina Berch (Dutton, 1988). *Biography of the fashion iconoclast Elizabeth Hawes: fashion designer, war worker, union organizer, and feminist.*

RARE BIRD OF FASHION: THE IRREVERENT IRIS APFEL
Eric Boman (Thames and Hudson, 2007). *A celebration of one of the most joyously stylish women fashion has ever known.*

ROOTS OF STYLE: WEAVING TOGETHER LIFE, LOVE, AND FASHION
Isabel Toledo (Celebra, 2012). *An autobiographical book by the elegant designer, illustrated by her husband, Ruben Toledo.*

SHOCKING LIFE
Elsa Schiaparelli (J. M. Dent and Sons, 1954). *The avant-garde designer (who refers to herself in the third person as "Schiap") writes her autobiography. She nearly tangos off the first dress she ever made; she turns down the chance to meet Mussolini; and she liked to visit Hamburger Heaven, buying a burger for herself and one for her daughter's dog, Popcorn.*

STRAPLESS: JOHN SINGER SARGENT AND THE FALL OF MADAME X
Deborah Davis (Tarcher/Putnam, 2003). *The story of Madame Gautreau, the Madame X of Sargent's painting, before and after the famous portrait.*

STYLE A TO ZOE: THE ART OF FASHION, BEAUTY, AND EVERYTHING GLAMOUR
Rachel Zoe, Rose Apodaca, Blanca Apodaca, and Donato Sardella (Hachette, 2007). *Rachel Zoe's book, the next best (or worst) thing to hiring her as your stylist. Expect Caftans.*

TALKING THROUGH MY HATS
Lily Daché (Coward-McCann, 1946). *The autobiography of famous milliner Lily Daché.*

THAT EXTRA HALF AN INCH: HAIR, HEELS AND EVERYTHING IN BETWEEN
Victoria Beckham and Hadley Freeman (HarperCollins, 2007). *Want to do anything like (Victoria) Beckham? This book is your chance.*

TOM FORD
Tom Ford (Rizzoli, 2008). *A catalog of Ford's design work for both Gucci and Yves Saint Laurent from 1994 to 2004, with more than three hundred photographs.*

VALENTINA: AMERICAN COUTURE AND THE CULT OF CELEBRITY
Kohle Yohannan (Rizzoli, 2009). *Wonderful overview of the dramatic career of Valentina, who dressed both Hepburns, Greta Garbo, and others.*

VALENTINO: THEMES AND VARIATIONS
Pamela Golbin (Rizzoli, 2008). *Catalog and accompanying material from the landmark exhibit of Valentino's work at the Museé des Arts Decoratifs.*

VOGUE: THE COVERS
Dodie Kazanjian (Abrams, 2011). *More than three hundred striking Vogue covers, with backstories.*

THE WEDDING DRESS: 300 YEARS OF BRIDAL FASHIONS
Edwina Ehrman (V&A Publishing, 2011). *Wedding dresses from 1700 to today, from the collection of the Victoria and Albert Museum. Includes Kate Middleton's dress.*

WHY IS A DRESS?
Elizabeth Hawes (Viking, 1942). *How to design dresses for women—not couture, mass production.*

WIFE DRESSING: THE FINE ART OF BEING A WELL-DRESSED WIFE
Anne Fogarty (Glitterati, 2008, new ed.). *Wonderfully quotable, if sometimes dated, book from the designer Anne Fogarty, including: "Personally, I don't think it's extravagant to have lots of shoes. I hate pedantic footwear."*

WOMEN OF FASHION: TWENTIETH-CENTURY DESIGNERS
Valerie Steele (Rizzoli, 1991). *Great women designers, and why there aren't more of them.*

YOHJI YAMAMOTO
Ligaya Salazar (V&A, 2011). *Interviews with the designer coupled with images from his own archive.*

YVES SAINT LAURENT
Florence Chenoune and Farid Muller (Abrams, 2010). *The accompanying volume to the Saint Laurent retrospective at the Petit Palais in Paris.*

A Note on the Author

ERIN MCKEAN is the author of the novel *The Secret Lives of Dresses*, inspired by her popular blog, A Dress a Day (dressaday.com), which features vintage clothes and patterns. A lexicographer by day and the founder of Wordnik.com, she has been published widely, including in the *New York Times Magazine* and the *Boston Globe*. She lives in the San Francisco Bay Area.

A Note on the Illustrator

DONNA MEHALKO is an artist and fashion illustrator who has worked for clients including Lord & Taylor, Henri Bendel, Revlon, and L'Oréal. She has also worked on projects with William Morrow, Farrar Straus & Giroux, and Viking Studio. She lives in New York City.

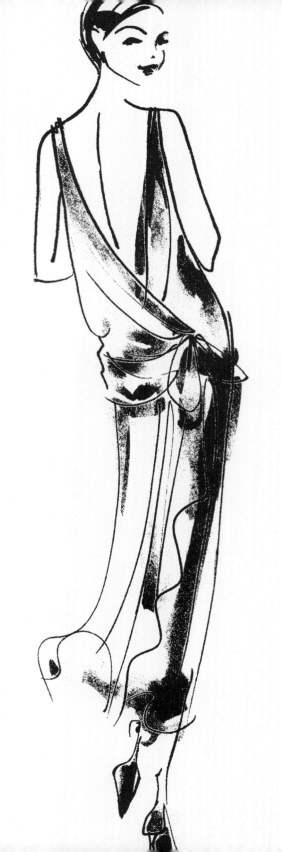